JOHN
MUIR

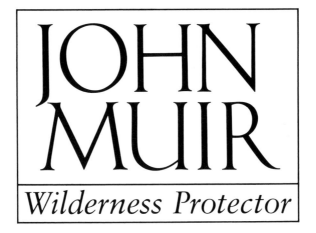

JOHN MUIR
Wilderness Protector

GINGER WADSWORTH

LERNER PUBLICATIONS COMPANY · MINNEAPOLIS

To Bill...
for believing

The author would like to extend special thanks to the following people
and organizations: Linda Eade and staff at the Yosemite Research
Library in Yosemite National Park; Daryl Morrison and staff at Holt-
Atherton Special Collections at the University of the Pacific; Pat Thomas
and staff at the John Muir Historical Site in Martinez, California; the
Bancroft Library at the University of California, Berkeley; Shirley
Sargent, author and historian; Bill and Maymie Kimes, Muir historians,
for their support and encouragement; Bill Wadsworth, for editing and
research assistance; and Susan Breckner Rose, my editor.

The sources for the quotes in this book can be found on pages 137-139.

LIBRARY OF CONGRESS CATALOGING-IN-PUBLICATION DATA

Wadsworth, Ginger.
    John Muir, wilderness protector / by Ginger Wadsworth.
        p.   cm.
    Includes bibliographical references and index.
    Summary: A biography of the naturalist and explorer who
helped found the Sierra Club and was influential in the development
of our national park system.
    ISBN 0-8225-4912-3
    1. Muir, John, 1838-1914—Juvenile literature. 2. Naturalists—
United States—Biography—Juvenile literature. 3. Conservationists—United States—Biography—Juvenile literature. [1. Muir,
John, 1838-1914. 2. Naturalists. 3. Conservationists.] I. Title.
QH31.M9W33   1992
508.794'092—dc20
[B]   91-35903
                                                                 CIP
                                                                  AC

Manufactured in the United States of America

1 2 3 4 5 6 7 8 9 10 01 00 99 98 97 96 95 94 93 92

Contents

The streets of Dunbar, Scotland, where John Muir played as a child

ONE

Racing across the Moors

1838–1849

On Saturday, 10-year-old Johnnie Muir wasted no time in getting outside. With his brother David and some of his friends, he scaled the crumbling walls of old Dunbar Castle. Johnnie felt his way up the walls by slipping his feet and hands into tiny cracks. Inch by inch, he scaled the 1,000-year-old walls and scrambled over the top. Behind him the North Sea pounded against the coast of Scotland.

Inside the damp castle, the boys darted from room to room, pretending they were soldiers from some past war. Their favorite section was down in the dungeon. Holding the stub of a candle, Johnnie went on ahead. He strutted through the cells and torture chambers carved in solid rock. Candle-light danced on the rough, dark walls. Feeling brave, he touched the moss-covered bones of a prisoner who had died long ago.

He dared the other children to follow him and touch the bones, too. Johnnie and the other boys liked these adventures and called their games "scootchers." Other times, they raced across the moors, but no one could run as fast as Johnnie Muir.

In 1833 Daniel Muir, a former army sergeant and a recent widower, married Anne Gilrye. The young couple lived in the rooms above his grain and food store in the town of Dunbar, east of Scotland's capital, Edinburgh. Daniel was a successful businessman noted for his honesty.

At that time, taxes were based on the number of windows in a house. To save on taxes, Daniel boarded up many of the windows so the house was gloomy inside. Anne did not complain, but learned to conform to her husband's wishes, as a good wife at that time was expected to. Tall and gray-eyed, she enjoyed nature and walks through the countryside. She liked to draw and paint and write poetry.

Daniel Muir belonged to the Gordon clan, a group of families descended from a common ancestor. At the age of 14, he had converted to a form of Christianity called Calvinism. Daniel joined a small group of evangelistic Presbyterians who believed that life was a constant struggle between God and Satan to possess a person's soul. To be saved, a person must worship God day and night, hour by hour. Daniel took these beliefs into his marriage and imposed them upon his children.

His first son, John, was born April 21, 1838. John had two older sisters: Margaret, born in 1834, and Sarah, born in 1836. David followed John in 1840 and Daniel, Jr., came next in 1843. In 1846 Anne Muir had twin daughters, Mary and Annie.

John, as the eldest son, developed an intense loyalty and concern for his brothers and sisters. Once, when his brother was about to be vaccinated, John jumped up and bit the doctor, yelling, "don't hurt my bonnie brither."

Although Daniel and Anne shared few interests, they enjoyed working in the garden behind their house, where they grew fruit trees and flowers. Daniel let his children plant seeds in the dry soil. John marveled at the way seeds produced leaves and flowers, and dreamed of having his own garden when he grew up.

Life in the Muir family revolved around Daniel. When he came home in a happy mood, everyone else was happy. For entertainment, Mr. Muir liked to sing or get out a fiddle he had whittled as a teenager. He played the wild dance tunes of his Highland ancestors. John and the rest of the children learned to dance and sing the old ballads that recounted the romances and stories of ancient Scotland.

Over the years, Mr. Muir changed from a religious man to a religious fanatic. He withdrew from the church that his wife and parents attended. He joined a new group, the Disciples of Christ, which had churches in Ireland, Scotland, and the United States.

Daniel Muir grew more serious and, by the time John was five or six, no longer allowed music—except hymn-singing—at home. He banned all art from the walls, forcing his wife to put away her needlework pictures. Whether at work or with his family, he quoted nonstop from the Bible. Many of the townspeople, including his father-in-law, thought Daniel Muir was too extreme concerning his religion.

During meals, no one could laugh, joke, or even talk. Daniel considered each meal a gift from God and therefore a solemn, serious experience. Anne learned to communicate with her seven children by signals—a quick smile or a raised eyebrow.

As a young child, John possessed an incredible amount of energy. He seemed to need more activities than his brothers and sisters. Grandfather Gilrye, Anne's father, became John's first teacher. Every day John, with his intense blue eyes and unruly russet-colored hair, pranced down the streets of Dunbar beside his grizzled, stooped grandfather. Grandfather pointed out the names of the letters and read the shop signs. John learned his numbers from the clock in the town square and was intrigued by how the clock worked. From that time on, he was fascinated with anything mechanical. Like his father, John was good with his hands. His grandfather helped him whittle toy ships and carve simple clocks. As he grew, John accompanied his grandfather far into the countryside where he learned to listen and look at the natural world.

John had started primary school at the age of three. His sisters Maggie and Sarah attended grammar school. He wore a kilt—a short, pleated, plaid skirt that is traditional for Scottish men and boys—and carried a bag around his neck that held his school books. Thanks to his grandfather, he already knew how to read.

Before leaving for school each day, John and the other children gulped down oatmeal porridge served in "luggies," little wooden tubs about four inches (10 centimeters) in diameter. Dinner was at noon. John rushed home for vegetable broth, a piece of boiled mutton, and a scone, or biscuit, made from barley flour. John was always hungry because his father believed that small, simple meals were good for the soul.

By the time he reached grammar school, John had learned that school "was founded on leather." The teachers used a tawse—leather straps fastened together—to discipline students. The boys were literally whipped into learning spelling, arithmetic, English, French, and Latin, plus geography and history.

John dreaded school and yearned to be outside. Because he learned quickly, he grew bored in the classroom. He drew ships and other pictures on the edges of his books. Like the other boys, he was enthralled with naturalist John James Audubon's stories of North American birds and with stories

The Muir family lived in the rooms above Daniel's food and grain store in Dunbar. Later the building became the Lorne Temperance Hotel.

about North American forests. He was especially fascinated with a maple tree that produced a sugary syrup.

Gold was discovered in California in 1848. John heard embellished tales of gold nuggets that miners gathered by the bucketful or picked out of river banks with their knives. America seemed like a paradise to John and his classmates.

In the school yard, the boys reenacted Scotland's wars with snowballs, sticks, dirt clods, or whatever they could find. The boys knew and loved Scotland's history and dreamed of becoming good fighters and joining the army. Johnnie and the other boys loved to fight even though their parents and teachers disapproved. A black eye meant a flogging at school and at home, but it was worth it.

After school, the family gathered for tea. Usually, they each ate a half slice of white bread, another barley scone, and a "cup of content"—warm water with a little milk and sugar.

Then John and David carried their schoolbooks to their grandparents' house across the street. The boys loved these evenings with their gentle grandparents. Grandfather listened to them recite their lessons in front of the warm fireplace. Sometimes they practiced French verbs or wrote compositions in Latin or French. Worried that her Johnnie was too thin, Grandmother Gilrye filled him up with oatmeal or caraway-seed cakes smothered with jam.

Back home, the boys joined the family for supper— usually a boiled potato and a piece of barley scone. Then came the long family worship, led by Daniel Muir. Each night, John had to recite a Bible verse or hymn by memory. He had a photographic memory and could memorize easily, if he remembered to look at the specific Bible passage. Anne Muir often quietly reminded her eldest son of his obligation so that he would not be punished. By the age of 10, John had memorized all of the Bible's New Testament and part of the Old Testament.

Even though it was late by the time family worship was over, the children revived upstairs and played games. Under their beds, they took imaginary around-the-world trips. Or they slipped into another room they believed belonged to a ghost. Once, John climbed out his dormer window and hung onto the sill as the wind billowed his nightshirt like a balloon.

On Saturdays, before his father stirred, John often escaped to join his friends even though he was expected to stay in the garden. Besides playing at Dunbar Castle, the boys held running matches up and down the hills for miles. At times, they ganged up to knock fruit off the trees and run through gardens. With his friends, John learned to swear, which angered his father.

Most of all, John loved to go to the seashore or the green fields to hear the birds sing or to hunt for nests. As the sun set, he headed home, knowing a thrashing was ahead. John knew that many of his friends would also get a beating from their fathers because that was the accepted form of discipline then.

Sometimes his mother was waiting at the door and quickly hurried him off to bed. But usually his father whipped him with a strap or a cane. John endured the pain. He enjoyed those "Saturday runaways" and knew that nothing would keep Johnnie Muir away from "Nature's glad wildness."

One night while David and John were studying at Grandfather's, their father burst through the door. In his Scottish brogue, he announced, "Bairns, you needna learn your lessons the nicht, for we're gan to America the morn!"

For Daniel Muir, the United States offered the most important opportunity in his life—religious freedom. Without consulting his wife, he had decided to farm in the United States and join a branch of the Disciples of Christ. He wanted land and great wealth to carry on his church's work.

After their father left the house, the boys danced around their grandparents' living room and chattered about finding gold, maple trees, and Audubon's birds. Later that evening, Grandfather handed each boy a gold piece for a keepsake. John wondered why Grandfather looked so solemn. It did not occur to him then that he would never see his grandfather again.

Daniel, Sarah, John, and David lived in this tiny shanty, above, *for a few months until Daniel finished building the white pine, frame house,* below, *on Fountain Lake for his entire family.*

TWO

Plowing the Fields

1849-1860

John, David, Sarah, and their father sailed for the United States in February 1849. Anne Muir stayed behind with the younger children, keeping 15-year-old Maggie to help her until a new home was ready.

Within a few hours of leaving Scotland, Sarah grew seasick and lay on her bunk for the entire six-week-long voyage. A few days later, Daniel Muir also became seasick. From then on, he only appeared on the main deck to attend prayer meetings or collect information about the United States.

But John and David had the time of their lives. No adults controlled them. John recalled that they "were on deck every day, not in the least seasick, watching the sailors at their rope-hauling and climbing work; joining in their songs, learning the names of the ropes and sails, and helping them as far as they would let us."

As they approached the coast of the United States, the boys spotted whales, dolphins, porpoises, and numerous seabirds. They learned their names and habits from the sailors.

During the trip, Daniel Muir heard about the abundance of rich farmland in Wisconsin. By riverboat, then by wagon, the Muir family headed west where Daniel filed a claim on 80 acres (32 hectares) of land, dotted with hickory and oak trees, near Portage, Wisconsin. John, David, and Sarah stayed with newfound friends while Daniel, neighbors, and a hired man constructed a one-window shanty. The little cabin overlooked a boggy, sloping meadow full of springs that fed into a lake. Daniel Muir named his land Fountain Lake Farm.

After the shanty was complete, the Muir children explored the farm for the first time. Eleven-year-old John jumped from the wagon. He had spied a blue jay's nest and shimmied up the tree to see the green speckled eggs inside. Then the boys raced down to the meadow. In the next few weeks, John and David found a bluebird's nest, then a woodpecker's nest in the woods. They discovered frogs, snakes, and turtles in the springs and spent hours searching through the grasses and brush for insects and animal burrows.

For the first few months, the boys had little to do but explore the wilderness. They acquired a puppy named Watch and a cat who soon had kittens. Mr. Muir bought the boys a pony named Jack. They learned to leap onto Jack's back and, without a saddle or bridle, guide the small horse by knee pressure or by shifting their weight. They galloped through the woods and often rode Jack to a big meadow to see sandhill cranes. Along the shore, they heard peepers sing. In later years, John wrote, "Here without knowing it we still were at school; every wild lesson a love lesson, not whipped but charmed into us. This sudden splash into pure wilderness—baptism in Nature's warm heart—how utterly happy it made us!"

During the summer and fall, the land had to be cleared quickly for planting. John and David helped the hired men burn brush in great fires. A team of oxen pulled the plow through sandy soil riddled with tree roots. The powerful animals hauled lumber for a permanent house on a hill.

Thirteen-year-old Sarah learned to cook meals on a woodburning stove instead of over an open fire as in Scotland.

John helped her haul water into the shanty. Chattering and arguing together, they washed the family clothes in a huge wooden tub using homemade lye soap that stung their eyes. Once in a while, Winnebago Indians, whose families had once lived on the land, appeared at the door to barter for food or sharpen their knives on the Muirs' grindstone.

Their new home was finished that October. Without frills such as pictures or fancy woodwork, the 2½-story house had eight rooms, a front hallway, and an entrance facing the road. Daniel Muir had used his money to build the finest house in the area. Sarah made curtains and planted a lilac bush at the front door. In the fields beyond, green shoots of winter wheat pushed through the soil.

Anne Muir arrived with Maggie, Danny, Mary, and Annie in early November. Within a month, deep snow blanketed the fields. High walls of snow shut in the house. John, who shared an attic bedroom and bed with his brothers, rose every morning at 6:00. Often the temperature reached -30°F (-35°C) as he forced his feet into frozen socks and boots and then went out to gather firewood. The kitchen stove provided the only source of heat in the house.

The men trudged to the barn to feed the animals. During rain and snowstorms, they remained in the barn to grind axes, shell corn, sort potatoes, or mend equipment. The women stayed in the house cooking and spent hours sewing or knitting.

The nearest neighbor lived 4 miles (6 km) away, and the closest town, Portage—a booming frontier town—was 12 miles (19 km) away. None of the children attended school.

Just before his 12th birthday the following spring, John was put to the plow. His head barely reached above the handles. As the eldest boy and the strongest, he also helped the hired men clear the fields by chopping down trees, then digging out the tree stumps. He split rails for zigzag fences. He could "cut and split a hundred a day...swinging the axe and heavy mallet, often with sore hands, from early morning to night." During the long, tedious hours, he escaped into his dreams, pondering beautiful whorls in hickory stumps or watching wood ducks glide across Fountain Lake.

At dusk, John brought in the cows and fed the livestock. He chopped firewood, sharpened tools, and carried buckets of water to the kitchen. Daniel Muir led the family in worship after supper. To stay awake during the long services, the children sometimes chewed strong-smelling windflower seeds.

During the summers when he was a teenager, John often rose at 4:00 in the morning and worked 14-hour days. David, Maggie, and Sarah were sent out to help John hoe the fields. Their father spaced them apart among the rows of potatoes and corn so they could not talk to each other.

The children dug their bare feet under the soil to keep the sun from burning their skin. They seldom went for a drink of water because the fields were in sight of the house and their father might flog them for leaving their work. Over and over again, Mr. Muir told his children, "You are God's property!"

Each August, Maggie and John reaped grain. As John felled the wheat in neat rows, and Maggie followed to bind the sheaves, the two children formed a deep friendship that would last the rest of their lives. One day they harvested six acres (2 hectares)—twice what most men could do. While working, John often saw squirrels scamper about in the oaks or noticed deer browsing at the edge of the field.

The children were only given two full holidays a year— New Year's Day and the Fourth of July. But occasionally, in

Anne Gilrye Muir, left, *and*
Daniel Muir, below

the evenings or on a Sunday afternoon, they were granted free time. They built a boat out of planks and sailed on the lake. John taught himself to swim by imitating the frogs and, at the same time, discovered an underwater world to study. The children explored the countryside with new neighbors — other recent immigrants from Scotland.

While his children worked the land, Daniel Muir preached — without pay — for the Disciples of Christ. Tall and stern-looking in his "Sunday blacks" with a fringed shawl of Gordon plaid and a black chimney-pot hat, he attended every revival and religious event he could. He grew famous for his 45-minute prayers and 90-minute sermons. As the neighbors said over the years, "He preferred preaching to working."

Daniel traveled in a wagon pulled by a pair of mares, Nob and Nell. John had grown attached to Nob, who was affectionate and intelligent. During one preaching excursion,

Daniel Muir pushed Nob to exhaustion. Back at the farm, John watched helplessly as the horse grew sicker and sicker and died of pneumonia a few weeks later.

On another occasion, Mr. Muir shot Watch, the family's dog. He believed Watch was eating chickens and sliced open the dog's stomach to prove it to his shocked children. Then he sold the pony, Jack, for a few coins to a traveler heading west. John later said, "There is one thing I hate with a perfect hatred—cruelty for anything or anybody!"

For a while, Daniel Muir adopted a diet of mostly graham bread and porridge. He decided that the family needed only one meal a day. Anne Muir and the girls were sick frequently. John nearly died of pneumonia. His father refused to send for a doctor, but instead prayed for John's recovery.

John was not afraid to argue with his father, so he complained about the unhealthy diet. To win his arguments, he often cited Bible passages. This time, he recounted the story of the prophet Elijah, who had ravens bring him meat while he hid from his enemies. Although Daniel Muir thought John was just "a lang-tongued chiel," he believed so strongly in the Bible that he allowed the family to eat meat again.

Even so, the new diet did not help Sarah and Maggie's health. They had already strained their bodies in the fields and would always suffer from poor health. Although a grown teenager at 5'9" (175 cm), John was shorter than his sisters and parents. He believed the hard labor and lack of food had stunted his growth.

Mrs. Muir taught her children to snatch every moment of pleasure, no matter how brief. When Mr. Muir was away preaching or praying, the family became a fun-loving group. They sang together, and John, with his endless energy, performed a series of Highland dances in the kitchen. Anne Muir

The Muir children were, top row, *Margaret, Sarah,* middle row, *John, David, Dan,* bottom row, *Mary, Annie, and Joanna.*

taught her daughters lace making and embroidery, but did not tell her husband. Sometimes, while the girls stitched, they listened to John read. His favorite authors were explorers Alexander von Humboldt and Mungo Park.

Over the years, many immigrant families—some of them fellow Disciples of Christ from Scotland—had settled in the area. One day, John joined several young men to build a community road. Some were teenagers like John; others were in their early twenties. As they worked, they recited poems by Shakespeare, Byron, Poe, Wordsworth, and Milton—poets John knew from his early school days. Years of drudgery fell from John's shoulders. He loved to read and was eager to learn more about the world.

Anne Muir, who had a reputation in the neighborhood as a "stay-at-home body," encouraged her eldest son to read and dream of traveling someday. She had inherited a small income from her father, which she always kept in a black bag on her arm. She handed out coins for such luxuries as hair ribbons, shawls, or new dresses for the girls. She probably helped John with his book buying, too.

When John was 17, his father bought a second farm, since wheat was in high demand. Because the Fountain Lake Farm had been continually planted with wheat instead of a succession of different crops, the soil had been depleted of nutrients. Daniel Muir wanted to make money for his church, to build orphanages, hospitals, and schools. If he had to sacrifice his children or destroy the land to do so, he believed that was the will of God.

Now Sarah and Maggie were expected to keep up Fountain Lake Farm. The other children worked the second farm, except Joanna, born in the early 1850s in Wisconsin and the favorite of Daniel Muir.

On the new farm, Hickory Hill, John began to prepare the land for planting. It disturbed him to uproot ancient hickory and oak trees and discard them at the edge of the fields. He worried about the birds and the other animals who had lost their food sources and homes.

It was a busy time. The family was packing to move into a newly built house on Hickory Hill. Sarah was about to be married. Her fiance, David Galloway, who had just returned to Wisconsin from a trip to Scotland, arranged to purchase the Fountain Lake Farm. Shocked by Sarah's haggard appearance, David vowed she would never work in a field again.

That spring, John began to dig for water at Hickory Hill. Mornings and afternoons, his brother David and his father lowered him by a bucket attached to a rope to the bottom of the well shaft. For months, he used a chisel and hammer to chip out the hard sandstone. He filled and refilled his bucket. One day, when the well shaft was about 80 feet (24 meters) deep, John grew faint. He slumped into the bucket and his father hauled him up. John had nearly died from carbonic acid gas, or what miners call choke damp.

William Duncan, a neighbor, taught the Muirs how to put a candle down into the shaft to find out if the air in the well contained enough oxygen for John to breathe. If the candle went out, the air in the well was unsafe.

Daniel Muir never spent an hour in the well. Instead, he let his son rest after his encounter with death. Two days later, he sent John down to finish the digging. Disturbed neighbors whispered among themselves that "Old Man Muir works his children like cattle."

Once again John returned to clearing the land. He vowed to leave home when he turned 21. "Living is more important than getting a living," he told his father.

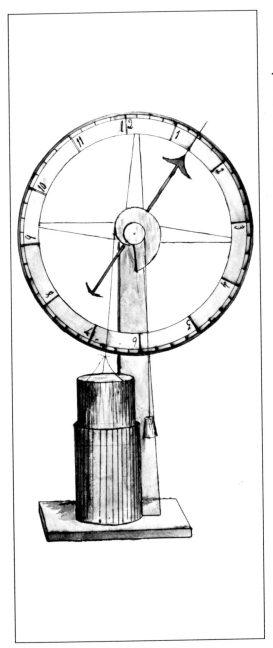

John designed many mechanical devices, including this clock. Impressed with his talent and persistence, his sisters expected him to become a famous inventor.

 **THREE**

Discovering Botany
1860–1864

John sought ways to relieve the long hours of tedious farm labor. He and his neighbors shared their small, well-worn collection of books. He used most every free minute to read, even while he walked the six miles (10 km) between the Hickory Hill and Fountain Lake farms. John persuaded his father to buy him an arithmetic book. He also taught himself algebra, geometry, and trigonometry.

Each night, the family worship service ended at 8:00 and John rushed to bed. He trained himself to wake up at 1:00 in the morning. He would tiptoe to the kitchen and light a candle, murmuring, "Five hours to myself! Five huge solid hours!" Sometimes he smuggled in borrowed novels to read in secret. He wrote poetry, too.

During the winter, it was usually too cold to read in the kitchen. John dared not light a fire and anger his father by wasting firewood. Instead, wrapped in thick layers of clothing, he tinkered with inventions by candlelight in the freezing cellar. With cold hands and using homemade tools, he built a self-starting sawmill with materials he uncovered in a junk pile in the cellar. Before long he had dammed a small brook to provide power and tried his sawmill successfully.

The machine age was dawning in the Midwest. John loved figuring out and designing mechanical solutions to make his life easier, but he loved nature equally. Confused by these conflicting interests, he walked the roads by moonlight to sort through his thoughts. He later wrote, "I used to spend hours with my head up in the sky. I soared among the planets and thoughts!"

William Duncan came to see John's inventions and lend him books. John had whittled a series of measuring instruments—barometers, hydrometers, and eventually clocks. Although John had never seen the inside of a clock, he had read a book about pendulum motion. His first clock, made of hickory wood and farm equipment, kept perfect time and struck the hours.

Once, Maggie discovered her father on his hands and knees studying John's clock. Mr. Muir did not like or understand the clock, or what his son was doing. Even so, he decided that 19-year-old John and the other boys could attend a nearby one-room school for a few months. For the first time since leaving Scotland, the boys went to school.

John began to live a more normal existence. He participated in and won spelling bees and, like many of the boys, admired the female students, including a "young female of eighteen with blue eyes and fair hair flowing." His sisters tried unsuccessfully to improve John's appearance because they said he looked "as wild as a loon."

He also had a sharp tongue due to years of constant arguing with his father. John took a certain pleasure in verbal combat with neighbors and classmates. Many of the neighbors called him odd and his inventions "freaks."

The year 1860 proved to be a turning point in John's life. He was 22 and restless. He wanted to leave as he had planned, but was reluctant to add additional burdens of farm work onto the rest of his family.

That summer, William Duncan brought him a newspaper with news of Wisconsin's State Agriculture Fair to be held in Madison in September. Duncan urged John to exhibit his inventions there, telling him that it might lead to a job in a machine shop. Now John had a reason to leave home.

After John's final silent meal with his family, Daniel Muir refused to say good-bye to his eldest son. John's mother and brothers and sisters cried.

John arrived by train in Madison, Wisconsin's capital, with $15, a few clothes, and his inventions. At the fairgrounds he set up his exhibits in the Temple of Art. Twenty thousand people thronged through the gates on opening day. One of the highlights of the exhibition was John's trick bed. Creaking wheels and levers raised the bed to a 45-degree angle and tipped the sleeper out of bed. One by one, eager children lined up to take their turn.

A front-page newspaper headline stated that John's inventions were the work of a genius. Before long, his exhibit was the main attraction at the fair. Thousands of people saw the young Scotsman in his shaggy beard and homespun clothes as he displayed his clocks, thermometer, and bed.

Jeanne Carr, one of the judges at the fair and the wife of a professor at the University of Wisconsin, met John at the fair and immediately recognized his talent. At the end of the fair, Mrs. Carr awarded the 22-year-old inventor a special cash prize. When word reached home, John's mother, brothers, and sisters were bursting with pride. Daniel Muir wrote his son a letter about the sin of vanity.

After the fair, John stayed in a Madison hotel doing odd jobs to earn his room and board. At first he was terribly shocked by young people who danced and even played kissing games. Yet everything intrigued him. Once, he climbed inside a piano to see how it worked. Mrs. Pelton, wife of the hotel owner, quickly befriended him and helped him adjust to Madison.

The presidential elections took place that fall, but John had learned little about national issues, for he had led an isolated life and still considered himself a Scot. Abraham Lincoln was elected president. People worried and talked about such issues as slavery and the right of the Southern states to secede, or separate, from the Northern states.

John liked to walk on College Hill in Madison. He gazed enviously at the University of Wisconsin buildings. In a casual conversation with a student, he learned how he might enroll. The acting dean agreed to register John as an "Irregular Gent."

Tuition for the 20-week-long semester was $10, and $6 covered room and board. For John, that was a lot of money. He moved into North Hall, the men's dormitory, in February 1861 and existed primarily on graham crackers, porridge, and water.

Many people knew John from the state fair. He continued to work on his inventions in his room and made a study desk that had a cogwheel to move his schoolbooks about, allowing a certain amount of study time per book. Students dropped in to his room to hear stories about Scotland. They also wanted to see and try his inventions, including his trick bed. Shelves of geological and botanical specimens lined his walls, and he rigged up his own chemistry lab. Sawdust and shavings littered the floor as John continued to whittle inventions.

He learned that botany—the study of plants and their scientific names—was a science. For him botanizing was sheer fun. In a letter to his sisters, he enthusiastically described some plants in his room. "I've got a fine posy at my

John sketched this
design for his desk,
which would only
allow him to study
one book for a certain
amount of time before
turning to the next
book.

The University of Wisconsin, Madison, circa 1870

nose in an old ink bottle. And I've got a peppermint plant and...on the shelf...stands my stew pan full of brambles 2 or 3 feet long."

The Civil War started in April 1861 after the shelling of Fort Sumter in South Carolina. Wisconsin was in an uproar. People attended rallies, speeches, and parades. Young men, including university students, dropped out of school to enlist in the military. John opposed fighting, recognizing that this was a real war, not a childhood game. To escape the constant war talk, he took long rambles in the hills or swam in the chilly waters of nearby Lake Mendota. He wrote to his sisters of reading on a tree bough overlooking the lake.

Despite the war and his unhealthy diet, John thrived in Madison. He found friendship and encouragement through the Carrs. Jeanne Carr, one of the social and intellectual leaders of Madison, was 12 years John's senior and the mother of two sons who adored John. She helped him bridge the gap from his isolated childhood to his new life. They talked frequently, for Mrs. Carr also loved nature. Religion was part of their dialogue, and John began to believe in a religion based on love, not fear as his father preached.

Professor Ezra Carr opened John's mind to the world of chemistry, but more importantly to geology. At the time, the study of the earth's history, its rocks and physical changes, was a new science. John read books on geology by Louis Agassiz and other scientists. Agassiz's teaching methods, as well as his theories on glaciers, were popular across the country, and John studied everything Agassiz wrote.

Professor Ezra Carr and his wife, Jeanne Carr, John's confidant and mentor

Another professor introduced him to the nature writings and philosophies of Henry David Thoreau and Ralph Waldo Emerson. Emerson's book entitled *Nature* impressed John. He began to keep a detailed journal to record his thoughts and observations, which he did for the rest of his life.

John blossomed in Madison. As one friend recalled, he was "straight as an arrow, with light hair, full beard, clear blue eyes and a skin smooth and transparent." He even had his first picture taken.

John went home in the summer of 1861. His father paid him 75¢ a day for his work on the farm. Even so, tensions remained between father and son. John saved his money, recognizing that the hard-earned wages would give him the freedom to return to the university.

When John returned to school in the fall, the fairgrounds had become a military camp where young men trained for war. Others had already died on battlefields. Many more lay sick and dying in hospitals. John thought about studying to become a doctor.

After another year at the university, he went home for a second summer. Maggie was married, his brother David was also a student at the university, and Danny was threatening to leave home. To everyone's surprise, Daniel Muir leased Hickory Hill Farm and moved the rest of the family into Portage. He allowed his children to go to school. Mrs. Muir subscribed to a Madison newspaper, telling John that "I think it is time we knew what is going on in the world."

John studied at the university for about 2½ years. Congress enacted a military draft, which meant that young men could be summoned to become soldiers. John qualified, but apparently was not called up. He was now 25. Friends and family encouraged him to marry and settle down.

John poses with his sister Sarah Muir Galloway and her two children in front of the Fountain Lake house in 1863.

He scribbled in a notebook that he was "tormented with soul hunger...[and]...began to doubt whether...[he] was fully born." To a friend he wrote, "I feel lonely again."

Instead of returning to school to study medicine, he took off alone for a long hiking trip in the Canadian wilderness. During the months he was away, he wrote little of why he left, or whether or not he was avoiding the military draft. His brother Dan was already in Canada. John tramped alone through miles and miles of wilderness, collecting plant specimens, eating a crust of bread at the end of the day, and sleeping wherever he found shelter.

One day John was hiking through a swamp. In a bed of yellow moss, he spied a single, pure white orchid—a calypso, the Hider of the North. John wrote of the beauty of the flower, so unexpected in the swamp. He sat beside the orchid and wept over the flower and his own loneliness.

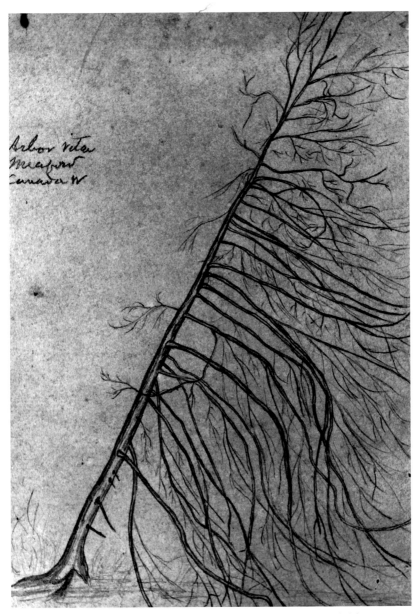

John was drawn to trees throughout his life. He sketched this arborvitae, or northern white cedar, in Meaford, Canada, in 1864.

·⸙⸙ FOUR ⸙⸙·

Walk to the Gulf

1864-1868

After months of wandering, John joined his brother Dan in the fall of 1864. They worked in a Canadian factory and sawmill—owned by William Trout—that produced rakes, brooms, and fork handles. John earned $10 a month, including room and board, as a mechanic.

Jeanne Carr wrote to John to suggest that they "exchange thoughts." They began to correspond. After Dan left in search of a better job, John grew lonely. He wrote that he feared an early death and dreaded he would not realize his many dreams. How would he find time to study botany, astronomy, geology, chemistry, and medicine if he spent his whole life as an inventor?

Day and night, his mind overflowed with ideas for labor-saving inventions. He tinkered with machine equipment and doubled the production of broom and rake handles. Instead of being happy with his success, he was confused about his future and wrote to Jeanne Carr that "I sometimes feel as though I was losing time here."

Two years later, a fire burned the factory to the ground, destroying John's labor-saving devices, plus 30,000 broom handles and 6,000 rakes. His nature notes and plant collection also burned in the fire. Trout was bankrupt and could only promise to pay John sometime in the future.

*John and Dan Muir were welcomed by the Trout family, whose
cabin near Meaford, Canada, is shown here in a sketch by John. The
two young men worked for the Trouts in their sawmill and factory.*

Now 28, John decided to return to the United States. He
found a job in a factory in Indianapolis, yet wrote to his sister
Sarah that "I feel something within, some restless fires that
urge me on in a way very different from my real wishes."
Homesick and lonely, he did not even unpack his trunk.

John rose early and worked long hours into the night.
His salary doubled, yet he dreamed of botanizing trips that
would lead him away from Indianapolis. He studied maps of
the southern United States, the West Indies, South America,
and Europe. He learned about tropical plants and trees, and
he wanted to see Florida, described as the "Land of Flowers."

After months of searching for a place to live, he became
a boarder with the Merrills, prominent members of the city.
The Merrills introduced John to their friends in Indianapolis,
as the Carrs had done in Madison. They encouraged John to
seek a patent for his inventions by registering them with the

government. John refused, saying that "the idea of it [his inventions] was really inspired by the Almighty."

He taught Sunday school in the gardens and fields surrounding the city, preferring to teach children about nature, instead of typical religious instruction. On other occasions, he spoke to the Merrills and their friends about the wilderness in Wisconsin and Canada. Everyone enjoyed listening to John, for he spoke easily and made each experience seem like an adventure. In one story, he wrote, "I had to sleep out without blankets, and also without supper or breakfast. But usually I had no great difficulty in finding a loaf of bread in the widely scattered clearings of the farmers. With one of those big backwoods loaves I was able to wander many a long, wild mile." On other days, he led hikes in the woods surrounding Indianapolis.

One night, as he worked late on a machine, tightening a newly installed belt with a file, his hand slipped. The tip of the file sprang into his right eye at the edge of the cornea. John touched his eye and felt the aqueous humor, the slippery material that protects and lubricates the working part of the eye, drip through his fingers. His vision failed quickly. John stumbled to bed, whispering, "My right eye is gone, closed forever on all God's beauty." The left eye soon failed, too, due to the extra stress.

Upon hearing the news, friends sent an eye specialist to examine John. The doctor assured him that his right eye would recover much of its function, and his left eye would return to normal. During his four weeks of bed rest, John talked with friends and pondered old plans to walk through the southern United States and then go to South America. He came across an illustrated brochure about California's Yosemite, a wilderness area in the snow-covered mountains of the Sierra Nevada. The brochure promised that Yosemite's cliffs and waterfalls were a "must" for tourists.

John did not talk of returning to the factory. When his eye had healed, and the aqueous humor was restored, he quit his job. Instead of working as a machinist and making inventions himself, he would spend the rest of his life studying "the inventions of God."

John traveled to Portage to say good-bye to his family. He first stayed with his sister Sarah and her husband, David Galloway. On a family picnic a few miles north of Portage, he discovered a tiny lake hidden and surrounded by a dense growth of small oaks, cattails, and blackberry vines. Like guard soldiers, rows of ferns ringed the lake; some were as tall as John. Immediately, he thought about how to preserve the little lake, which he named Fern Lake. His idea of preserving land in its natural state began that day.

In August 1867, John prepared to walk through the southeastern states and make his way to South America. The parting from his family was bittersweet. John had the feeling that this leave-taking would be real. Daniel Muir asked his son to pay for his lodging. John handed over a gold piece—perhaps the one his grandfather had given him nearly 20 years before—and told him, "You may be very sure it will be a long time before I come again."

On the road, John penned an informal will to his brother Dan. He parceled out his possessions, leaving nothing to his father. Later in life he reminisced, "I could have become a millionaire [because of the inventions] and I chose to become a tramp."

He took off, carrying maps and a compass. John wanted to take the "wildest, leafiest, and least trodden way." In Kentucky, he saw magnificent oaks, explored caves, and followed

As John walked through Georgia, he saw the devastation wreaked by the Civil War. Shown here is a street in Atlanta.

the paths of such earlier explorers as Daniel Boone. He made his first entry in his journal, "John Muir, Earth-planet, Universe."

John traveled with only the gray suit he wore, a plant press, some toilet articles, a change of underwear, and three books: the New Testament, Milton's *Paradise Lost*, and the poetry of Robert Burns.

Every morning, John rose with anticipation of the adventures ahead. He walked about 25 miles (40 km) a day, eventually going over 1,000 miles (1,600 km). He encountered the men and women who had recently been freed from slavery. He saw poverty all around him—empty fields, burnt factories, abandoned homes, overgrown roads—the results of the Civil War.

John watched for roving bands of robbers. With his weathered face and untrimmed hair and beard, he was not bothered much. He resembled a poor herb doctor, with plants trailing from his press and pack. Sometimes he slept under a tree or dozed on a hillside, "muttering praises to the happy abounding beauty" of the country. Once, he slept on a bench in a schoolhouse.

In Tennessee, he reached the Cumberland Mountains, the first mountains he had ever seen. He scrambled to the top of a peak to see North Carolina and Georgia. Each day he eagerly studied the birds, listened to their songs, collected plants, and observed all kinds of insects and animals. He wrote in his journal, added sketches, then slipped the leather-bound volume in his coat pocket.

Days later he reached Georgia, following the Savannah River, passing great cypress swamps. He saw alligators for the first time. Hungry, thirsty, and feeling feverish at times, John finally reached the city of Savannah where his brother had been told to send him letters and money.

In Savannah, no package had arrived. John had money for crackers, but not a hotel. He wandered away from town, past the ruins of a white-pillared mansion near a rundown cemetery. He stayed among the tombs and the oaks, which trailed Spanish moss. The first night, he slept with his head on a grave and commented, "my sleep had not been quite so sound as that of the person below."

For five or six days, he grew even thinner as he waited for news and money from home. He built a shelter with bushes, rushes, and a carpet of moss in the midst of the gravestones. Inside his little bower, he wrote in his journal for hours, capturing his feelings about God, humanity, life, and death. Of death he wrote, "But let children walk with Nature, let them see the beautiful blendings and communions of death and life...and they will learn that death is stingless indeed, and as beautiful as life, and that the grave has no victory, for it never fights. All is divine harmony."

John had 25¢ left when his money finally arrived. He immediately devoured a tray of gingerbread from a Savannah street vendor, then an entire dinner in a market. Although still feverish, he took a boat to Florida. He walked through Florida, finding the tropical plants he had read about and come to see. In a swamp, he discovered a palmetto, a palm tree with fan-shaped leaves. Each plant discovery was like meeting a new friend, and he recorded that "this palm...told me grander things than I ever got from a human priest."

On the gulf coast of Florida, he walked the beaches in his worn suit and thought about his early days in Scotland. He swam in the surf and wondered why he was so tired. One day, while searching for plants along a trail, he fell unconscious and was found by some local residents. For the next three months, John battled malaria, a disease accompanied by chills, fever, and sweating. He nearly died. John recovered slowly, staying with new friends, writing in his journal, sketching, and taking quinine to treat the malaria.

Although still frail, John booked a passage to Cuba on the *Island Belle* in 1868. The schooner anchored in the harbor of the Cuban capital, Havana. Every day, John rowed to shore. Along the beach, he gathered shells. Inland, he discovered cactus, swamps, and vines. He dreamed of traveling farther south, of seeing Colombia and Venezuela, of going up the Amazon River, but the fever kept returning. And no ships stopped en route to South America.

John decided to return to the United States. He took a steamer to New York. In New York's busy harbor, he purchased a berth on a ship sailing for California. Although weak and low on funds, John decided to explore Yosemite.

Overhanging Rock at Glacier Point above Yosemite Valley

$\cdot$ ➤➤ FIVE ➤➤ $\cdot$

Of Yosemite Magnitudes

1868-1870

A few weeks before his 30th birthday, and nearly 20 years after the gold rush had begun in California, John sailed into San Francisco Bay. More than 150,000 miners, fortune seekers, and other citizens packed the city in 1868. John sought the quickest route out of town.

He set off with a shipmate. His eventual destination was Yosemite Valley. Southeast of San Francisco, he climbed Pacheco Pass. At the summit, John paused. What he saw ahead took his breath away. For hundreds of miles beyond the pass stretched the snowcapped Sierra Nevada "in glorious ranks and groups, their snowy robes smooth and bright." He could see about 400 miles (650 km) of the mountains—the longest, highest, and grandest single range in the United States.

John was in no hurry. With every step, his health and spirits improved. Descending from the pass, he and his companion zigzagged leisurely through the San Joaquin Valley—a large, wide plain. Small streams and the San Joaquin River crisscrossed the rich soil.

The two young men passed wheat and alfalfa fields. Farmers tended orchards and vineyards. In some places, the valley was a sea of purple lupine and yellow poppies. Knee-deep in flowers, John studied the plants with his magnifying

lens and pressed specimens in his plant press. John wrote
to Jeanne Carr that, "here [the flowers] are not sprinkled
apart with grass between... but grasses are sprinkled among
the flowers."

Eventually the two men trekked up the green, rounded,
oak-covered foothills that led to the mountains. After several
days, they reached the rim of Yosemite Valley. From a distance, John saw Bridalveil Fall blowing sideways in the wind.

Bridalveil Fall

*Half Dome looms above the bed of the Merced River in
Yosemite Valley.*

He knew that the Native Americans called the place "Pohono,"
or spirit of the puffing wind. At first he called it a "dainty
little fall...only about fifteen or twenty feet high." John laughed
after discovering that Bridalveil Fall drops 620 feet (190 m).
"So little did we know of Yosemite magnitudes!"

Travel into the canyon was by mule or on foot. At times,
as the two men created their own route into the canyon, they
hiked through deep snow. For John, the floor of the valley—
seven miles (11 km) long and one mile (1½ km) wide—resembled a lush green garden. Rock walls, which tower up to
3,000 feet (915 m) high, ring the valley. The Merced River—
River of Mercy—meanders through the middle.

John kept no journal during this brief visit, but wrote later that "the magnitude of the mountains are so great that unless seen…a good long time they are not seen nor felt at all." The Yosemite Valley was "the grandest of all the special temples of Nature I was ever permitted to enter."

He spent about 10 days in the area and added to his plant collection. Hoarding his last cash, John lived primarily on tea and flour. He tasted bear meat once but disliked the oily, rank flavor. At the Mariposa Grove, he walked awestruck among the cinnamon-colored trunks of more than 600 sequoias, the largest trees in the world.

Needing money, John returned to the San Joaquin Valley. He harvested crops, broke horses, ran a river ferry, and became a sheep herder. In his journal, he pondered, "What shall I do? Where shall I go?" He worked long hours beneath the clear blue sky and wrote to his brother David that "farming was a grim, material, debasing pursuit under Father's generalship. But I think much more favorably of it now."

During the winter and into the spring of 1869, John was primarily a sheep herder. But in his spare time, he continued to teach himself about plants; watch the ever-changing weather; study birds, reptiles, and insects; and read Shakespeare. He often sang old Scottish ballads. After a spring rain, he went "to meet the lovely visitors [the flowers] in their robes of gold. I welcomed them to the world, congratulated them on the goodness of their home, and blessed them for their beauty."

He sent money home. His sister Mary had fled to live with her married sisters. Daniel Muir had flung his daughter's watercolor drawings into a mud puddle and stomped on them to save her soul. John, who recognized her artistic talent, encouraged Mary to study art, music, and botany at the University of Wisconsin. He wrote to the Carrs as well, for they were moving to the San Francisco Bay area. Dr. Carr would teach agriculture at the University of California.

With a small crew, John herded 2,000 sheep toward the green mountain pastures. Before long he called the sheep "hoofed locusts" because they ate and trampled everything in their path. John recorded these and other thoughts in a notebook that dangled from his belt by a leather thong. When he could, he penciled in sketches. He added, "We are now in the mountains and they are in us, kindling enthusiasm, making every nerve quiver, filling every pore and cell of us." He wrote of becoming a mountaineer, though unsure of what that meant. As he told his brother Dan, he wanted to witness all of nature's doings.

While the sheep grazed north of Yosemite Valley in Tuolumne Meadows—at an elevation of 8,575 feet (2,614 m),

"Hoofed locusts" graze in Tuolumne Meadows.

John sketched Half Dome showing beyond a bend in the Merced River.

the largest subalpine meadow in the Sierra Nevada—John immersed himself in the land. He was happier than he had been since his first summer in Wisconsin. He learned to bake bread on a piece of bark over an open fire. After doing other daily chores, he continued to botanize and climb many of the peaks. In his journal, he wrote, "I feel sure I should not have one dull moment."

One night he slept on a rock in the middle of a stream; other nights he gazed at stars and listened to the wind in the trees. He measured pinecones and followed bear tracks. Lying

At a slightly different bend in the river, Half Dome is visible on the right and North Dome is on the left.

on his stomach, he observed sprouting seeds through his hand lens. As in his early days in Scotland, he scrambled up trees. Once, his wild bursts of singing scared a brown bear from a thicket of berries.

He liked to sit or stand on the helmet-shaped summit of North Dome, which overlooks the upper end of Yosemite Valley. Beyond looms Half Dome, the valley's most dominant feature—1,300 feet (400 m) higher than North Dome, one face a 2,200-foot (670-m) sheer granite cliff. Looking east, John saw more domes, peaks, and forested slopes. To Sarah

Yosemite Falls

he wrote, "I am a captive, I am bound. Love of pure unblemished Nature seems to overmaster and blur out of sight all other objects and considerations."

Unusual landforms, like North Dome, fascinated him. From his rock perch, he saw canyons and valleys that he believed had been carved by ancient glaciers—large, slow-moving sheets of ice that push rocks and debris and gradually gouge the earth underneath.

He was equally intrigued by the thundering waterfalls that plunged over the cliffs and twisted through wild canyons into the valley. One day, at Yosemite Falls, John crept barefoot to the edge of the fast-moving, icy waters. He wanted to see North America's highest waterfall as it plummeted 2,400 feet (730 m) to the valley below. Ahead he saw a tiny ledge and inched along 20 or 30 feet (6 or 9 m) until he could look directly "down into the heart of the snowy, chanting throng of comet-like streamers." Water was above, below, and beside him; spray drenched him.

John's sketch entitled "From back of foot of Lower Yosemite Fall"

He had no sense of time, no memory of returning to safety and putting on his shoes. It was a death-defying experience, the first of others to come. John believed he had subconscious wisdom, more powerful than his sense of reason, which would advise him if he were in danger.

Tiring of the sheep, John and Harry Randall, a young ranch hand, found work in Yosemite Valley. About 1,000 tourists traveled to Yosemite each year, but the existing hotels were primitive. The new transcontinental railroad had opened in 1869, bringing easterners to California. Five years earlier, Abraham Lincoln had signed a grant to set aside the Yosemite Valley and Mariposa Grove for public use and recreation. No

John sketched the tourists camping in Yosemite Valley.

industry could use the area. California's legislature accepted the grant in 1866, creating the first wilderness park in the United States. However, no government protection existed for areas beyond the 40,000-acre (16,000-hectare) park.

James M. Hutchings, a hotel keeper, hired John to build a sawmill to cut lumber for new cottages. A large number of pines and oaks had fallen in a powerful windstorm. John would use these downed trees with Harry Randall's help.

Before starting the mill, John built a one-room cabin of sugar pine shakes with a floor of round tree slabs. He spaced the slabs so ferns below might unfurl in the spring and he "brought a stream into the cabin entering at one end with just current enough to allow it to sing and warble in low, sweet tones, delightful at night while I lay in bed." From their hammocks, Harry and John peered out their only window at Yosemite Falls.

During the next year, John, who enjoyed companionship and loved to give nature lessons, taught Harry botany and geology and led him on long hikes. As their friends discovered, it was hard to keep up with the wiry Scotsman. Often creating his own trails, John pushed through heavy brush, forded streams, and with the skill of an athlete, leaped easily from boulder to boulder. Always unpredictable, he might leave the trail to greet a flower or follow a fawn. His idea of an easy two-day saunter was 50 miles (80 km).

As he built the sawmill and began construction of the cottages, John stuffed his pockets with bark, mosses, and other bits of nature from the fallen trees. At night he studied his treasures on a homemade desk in his cabin. He was learning about the close relationships in the natural world and wrote, "When we try to pick out anything in nature, we find it hitched to everything else in the universe."

Glaciers are large bodies of ice that, as they move slowly downhill, carve out the land under them with their weight. John made this sketch to show how the movement of prehistoric glaciers might have carved out Half Dome.

In lengthy letters to friends and family, John shared his discoveries and enthusiasm. He began to study glaciers with the same patience and persistence he had applied to his inventions. He seldom slept more than a few hours a day. In his free time, John clambered above the valley to prove his own glacial theories, which were quite different from those of the state's expert, Josiah Whitney.

Whitney, head of the California Geological Survey and a professor of geology from Harvard University, stated that glaciers were not a major factor in creating the landscape. He believed that Yosemite Valley had been created by violent forces, such as an earthquake.

John, however, had come to believe that ancient glaciers had scored and polished the granite domes and walls, carved out the lakes, and shaped the valleys. He discovered rocks and boulders lacerated by glacial ice. He examined the cuts with his hand lens. On other outings, he inspected the moraines, or hills formed of earth and rocks transported by glaciers. Many boulders were of a different color and composition, as though they had been carried from far away.

John also believed that glaciers still existed and were not just a thing of the past. To continually test his theory, he set out lines and stakes to measure any movement of ice that might be a glacier. He kept careful notes and illustrations.

Jeanne Carr encouraged John to speak out. She had read his many letters on glaciation and knew of his detailed research. John was reluctant at first. He was only a mill hand and tour guide, not a prominent scientist like Josiah Whitney. John thought about it some more. He decided to talk about his findings. After all, he had no reputation to lose, and he wanted to be true to himself.

One morning, while acting as a guide, he told a group of listeners, "I can show the Professor [Whitney] where the mighty cavity [the Yosemite Valley] had been grooved and wrought out for millions of years. I can take you where you can see for yourself how the glaciers have labored, and cut and carved."

John often retreated from the tourists and went hiking. Here he sits at the foot of Vernal Fall.

SIX

Glaciers
and an Earthquake

1870-1873

With encouragement from Jeanne Carr and others, John continued to talk about his discoveries. Impressed visitors listened, recognizing that John disagreed strongly with Josiah Whitney's theories. At once John was in the center of controversy. Whitney, who labeled John an "ignoramus," refused to reevaluate his own position on glaciation.

Tourists arrived daily in the Yosemite Valley. John grumbled about taking time off from the mill and his nature studies to be a tour guide. He resented some of the visitors, especially the women in fancy dresses who squealed at the sight of a snake and refused to venture beyond the valley floor.

For a while, Therese Yelverton, who claimed to be an Irish countess, pursued John. She followed the blue-eyed mill worker and recorded his every word.

During this time, however, John's strongest relationship was with Jeanne Carr. He read constantly for she shipped him a steady supply of books. Their letters poured back and forth between the San Francisco Bay area and Yosemite. John even penned some with ink made from sequoia tree sap. In one letter, Mrs. Carr asked John to come to the city to be "polished." She worried about his isolated life. John would not budge. He loved Yosemite and wanted to learn all he could about "God's mountains."

Convinced of John's uniqueness and genius, Mrs. Carr sent her friends to meet the young Scot. In August 1870, Joseph Le Conte, professor of geology at the University of California, arrived at the mill to talk to John.

They talked excitedly about glaciers. Le Conte was immediately swayed by John's expert understanding of geology and wanted to see the evidence of glaciers firsthand. John hurriedly packed a small bag of food—oatmeal, tea, cheese, dried beef, and crackers—and put on his broad-brimmed hat. The mill could wait.

For several days, the two men traveled by horseback into the mountains surrounding Yosemite Valley. They talked and gestured constantly, exchanging information. One evening, Le Conte wrote in his journal that, like John Muir, he believed a glacier once filled Yosemite Valley. He praised "Muir's discovery" and added that "Mr. Muir...is the most passionate lover of Nature. I think he would pine away in a city or in conventional life of any kind." The two men parted as friends, promising to stay in touch.

Tired of the persistent Countess Yelverton, John fled the valley. The countess left too and, the following year, published a novel called *Zanita* set in a Yosemite-like locale. The main character, Kenmuir, strongly resembled John Muir.

John returned. In January 1871, he built a small, box-like home—six feet (2 m) by eight feet (2½ m)—fastened beneath the gable of the mill and jutting over a stream. A skylight in the roof faced Yosemite Falls. John named his new home his "hang-nest."

He continued to explore and read "new chapters of glacial manuscript" by going to the high country to examine glaciers.

It was time-consuming work to set out stakes to measure their slow movement.

Not only did John study glaciers, but everything in nature. For long trips, John packed a mule named Brownie with canvas bags filled with blankets and food. He did not carry a rifle, believing that he should not kill the animals he was learning about.

John wore a woolen shirt and baggy pants that would not interfere with his walking. He stuffed a vest with such

In this view of Yosemite Valley, the highest point on the left is El Capitan, the peak in the middle is Half Dome, the highest point on the right is one of the Cathedral Rocks, and below it is Bridalveil Fall.

John planted stakes in Lyell Glacier, shown here, to measure its movement. He found that the sides of a glacier flow more slowly than the center.

things as a compass and a pocket knife. Instead of boots, he liked ankle-high shoes shod with round-headed nails.

Leading Brownie, he squeezed between narrow rocks, pushed through thick brush on faint animal trails, or created new paths. The sure-footed mule learned to leap among the boulders and cross icy streams. As long as there was grass for Brownie and bread for John, the two might stay out for weeks at a time.

At night by the fire, John wrote in his journal, then went to sleep on a bed of fir boughs under the stars. He lay near a stream to listen to its song. Brownie would bolt if a bear came near the campsite, but John always found the mule in the morning.

On other trips, when the terrain was unusually rough, John tethered Brownie back at the hang-nest. He carried a sack of food at his waist to free his hands for climbing, leaving behind his coat and blankets. During the long, lonely, cold nights, he huddled near a blazing fire.

At the end of one extended trip, he ran into a huge snowstorm. He formed snowshoes from bark and hiked back to the valley. His clothes hung in tatters and his hair needed combing. To protect his skin from windburn, John smeared his face with charcoal. When he first arrived home, he scared the valley children with his wild looks.

In May 1871, John met Ralph Waldo Emerson. The Sage of New England, who had impressed John and so many others with his writings on human nature and the natural world, visited Yosemite. The 68-year-old philosopher climbed the sloping plank ladder into John's hang-nest. John, who was just 33, was awed and honored that Emerson wanted to see his plants, rock collections, maps, and sketches.

For the next few days, they talked often. John acted as a tour guide. They parted in Mariposa Grove, after Emerson named a giant sequoia Samoset in honor of a Native American leader. Emerson's friendship and approval strengthened John. He wrote, "I will follow my instinct, be myself for good or ill, and see what will be the upshot. As long as I live, I'll hear waterfalls and birds and winds sing. I'll interpret the rocks, learn the language of flood, storm, and the avalanche. I'll acquaint myself with the glaciers and wild gardens, and get as near the heart of the world as I can."

To his companions, Emerson later said, "There is a young man from whom we shall hear," and he urged John to return to society. But John was not ready for city life. Instead, during his solitary travels into the woods, John carried Emerson's essays and read them by firelight.

John began a systematic exploration of the canyons. He checked his stakes and added to his botanical collection. Too busy and excited to work at the mill, he quit to study nature full time. He had saved $500 and that would have to do.

At one site in the Merced Range, he found a stream that carried away a fine gray mud of ground-up granite. He picked up the freshly ground glacial earth. John shouted, "Glacial mud! A living glacier!" He raced up the precipice until he stood at the head of the slow-moving ice. Here was proof! Glaciers did exist! John shouted his joy to the sky. During the next two years, John discovered and measured the movements of 65 small glaciers.

For several years, he had toyed with writing up his findings for publication. Jeanne Carr encouraged him. She even suggested titles and copied his notes. Although writing did not come naturally to him, John decided to send an article to the *New York Tribune*. To his surprise, the newspaper published "Yosemite Glaciers" on December 5, 1871, and paid him $200—a lot of money then. On New Year's Day in 1872, the same newspaper printed "Yosemite in Winter." John thought he might be able to earn his living by writing, what he called "pen work." He holed up in his cabin for the winter.

One night in March, he was awakened by an earthquake. Frightened at first, John raced into the moonlit meadows. He watched Eagle Rock, a rock spire on the south wall of the valley, topple to the ground. Boulders plummeted everywhere; the noise was deafening. Before the dust had settled, John was leaping among the debris, shouting, "A noble earthquake, a noble earthquake!"

Later he joined his valley neighbors and suggested they "smile a little and clap your hands. Mother Earth is only trotting us on her knee to amuse us and make us good!" No one was amused. Everyone thought John Muir was a little crazy.

In the months following the earthquake, John sold two articles to the popular Pacific Coast magazine, *Overland Monthly*. His reputation grew. World-renowned scientists began to call on the woodsman in Yosemite to learn from him and encourage him to continue his research.

That fall John met a Scotsman, William Keith, who came to Yosemite with a letter of introduction from Jeanne Carr. Keith, a landscape artist, was the same age as John. Before the day had ended, they were calling each other Johnnie and Willie and swapping stories about Scotland. Keith, who had lived in cities most of his life, asked John for a good painting

William Keith probably painted this view of the cascades near the head of the Tuolumne River on his first trip with John.

While Keith was painting, John climbed Mount Ritter. He felt this climb would help him understand all other mountains because of its difficulty.

site. A few days later, John led Keith and his friends to a scenic spot on the Tuolumne River.

John left the group and spent a few days climbing Mount Ritter, something he had long wanted to do. Over the years, he had perfected his mountaineering techniques. Mount Ritter, with its summit of 13,157 feet (4,010 m), was considered inaccessible because of its steep glacial walls and deep canyons.

Alone, he set up a base camp at 11,000 feet (3,400 m). That night he built a blazing fire and slept on a rock. He stoked the fire often to stay warm. At dawn he dined on tea and oatmeal cooked in a can with a wire handle. He left his coat behind, not wanting it to flap in the wind or snag while he climbed.

Challenged by the dangers, John began to scale the dark wall, hammering away chunks of ice with a small ax. Knobs and fissures for his feet and fingers became fewer and farther between. Then, clinging to the rock face with arms outstretched, he froze. Absolutely panicked, he feared he would fall.

He gripped his hand and toe holds for a few minutes until, suddenly, he visualized the climb ahead. "Every rift, flaw, niche and tablet in the cliff ahead, were seen as through a microscope. At any rate the danger was safely passed...and shortly after noon I leaped...upon the highest crag of the summit."

Standing on the top of Mount Ritter, he spotted dozens of familiar landmarks: Mount Whitney, the San Joaquin Valley, and Mono Lake. Before dark he climbed down using a different route.

Two months later, John traveled to Oakland for a brief visit with the Carrs, and with new friends like the Le Contes and the Keiths. John ferried back and forth between San Francisco and Oakland, taking streetcars to galleries, libraries, and museums. He walked on hard pavement. He even attended a seance. Everyone wanted to entertain him.

Despite the diversions, he longed for the peace of the mountains. After two miserable weeks, he boarded an eastbound train. He disembarked in the town of Turlock and hurried as fast as he could back to Yosemite.

Self-portrait of John exploring the Sierra Nevada

SEVEN

Courtship
1873-1880

Before winter snows blanketed the mountains in 1873, John explored the southern Sierra Nevada. He walked more than 1,000 miles (1,600 km) throughout the mountains during the fall, and finally traveled back to Oakland. To his sister Sarah he wrote, "I find this literary business very irksome, yet I will try to learn it."

Encouraged by friends, John had decided to publish what he knew about the Sierra Nevada. He had two purposes: "to entice people to look at nature's loveliness" and to teach people to take care of the natural world.

John needed to spend time in the San Francisco area to meet editors at the *Overland Monthly* and to use references not available in the mountains. Because the Carrs were mourning the death of their eldest son, John moved in with other friends. Even so, the Carrs wanted to introduce John to "society." Jeanne Carr especially wanted John to meet the Strentzels.

Dr. John Strentzel, a Polish exile, a wealthy landowner, and a fruit grower, lived east of Oakland in the Alhambra Valley near the town of Martinez. Strentzel, his wife Louisiana, and their daughter, Louie Wanda, were friends of the Carrs.

Mrs. Carr made no secret of her interest in matching Louie with John. Louie, who was in her late twenties, had graduated from Miss Atkins Seminary in Benicia—now Mills College in Oakland. Louie often took the train to San Francisco to shop and visit friends. A gifted musician, she gave up a chance to be a concert pianist to stay with her parents. She maintained an elaborate flower garden and did the bookkeeping for her father's ranch. Mrs. Carr thought Louie and John would have much in common. But John escaped for long walks whenever Mrs. Carr tried to bring them together.

John began to spend his days writing. He had already started a series of essays on his glacial theories. Although he loved to write long, lively letters to his friends and family, he soon discovered that writing articles for publication was "like the life of a glacier—one eternal grind."

The first of his "Sierra Studies" appeared in the May 1874 issue of *Overland Monthly*. A wide range of readers eagerly looked forward to more. Before long John became the magazine's leading contributor. After nearly a year of writing and city life, John put down his pen and announced, "The Mountains are calling me and I must go." He had had enough of rich food, parties, and the noises and smells of the city.

He refreshed his spirit at his favorite Yosemite haunts. For the next few months, he walked hundreds of miles. He viewed the clear blue waters of Lake Tahoe on the border between California and Nevada. He went south to Mono Lake, an ancient and unusual-looking lake where towerlike calcium formations dot the shore. Next he circled north toward Mount Shasta, a lone mountain that rises 14,162 feet (4,317 m) above sea level.

John, the mountaineer, could not resist the attraction of this inactive volcano. For a month, he explored Mount Shasta's glaciers and glacial channels, circling the base and eventually climbing to the top twice. He reported on his travels through

John told the Swett children about the time he was trapped on Mount Shasta during a storm. On the morning after the storm, his feet were frostbitten and he could not walk, so his friends had to hoist him onto his horse.

letters, which appeared in a San Francisco newspaper, the *Bulletin*.

For the next five years, his life assumed a pattern. In the summers, he was off exploring, while during the winters he rented a room in John and Mary Swett's home in San Francisco. John Swett, a former California state superintendent of education and a published author, now worked as a school principal.

John loved the Swetts' large, noisy household. He missed his own family in Wisconsin. Daniel Muir had sold the farm and moved to Canada. He had joined a Disciples of Christ group that visited the sick and dying in hospitals. Although not legally separated from him, Anne Muir remained in Portage, Wisconsin, near her children and grandchildren.

During the winter, the Swetts' little toddler, Helen, often played at John's feet as he sat writing at his desk. A natural storyteller, John enjoyed entertaining Helen and the three older Swett "bairns" with his animal stories. They refused to go to bed until "Uncle John" gathered them around the fireplace and told them stories, including one about a pack rat who stole his barometer, and another about entertaining some Douglas squirrels with Scottish tunes.

After hearing one bedtime story about a snowstorm on Mount Shasta, in which John suffered frostbitten feet, the Swetts insisted that he hurry upstairs to write the experience exactly as he had told it to the children. John did and, gradually, began to capture these stories in his own voice.

He sold "The Humming Bird of the California Waterfalls" to *Scribner's Monthly* in 1878. The "humming bird" was really

In later years, John Swett, left, and John Muir, right, would meet each morning on the border between their ranches and walk up to the Swetts' porch, where they discussed the problems of the world.

John loved the wildness of storms in Yosemite Valley and reveled in the music of the wild wind and the smell of the rain.

a water ouzel, a stream-loving bird that ducks underwater for food. The story was popular across the country. John decided to submit "Wind-storm in the Forests of the Yuba."

In "Wind-storm" he wrote about the violent side of nature, which he also loved. Once, he climbed to the top of a 100-foot (30-m) Douglas fir during a gale. With his coat whipping about him, John clung to the arching tree and savored the storm, especially the musical sounds of the wind rushing by. He wrote that "it never occurred to me until this storm-day, while swinging in the wind, that trees are travelers...[and]...our own little journeys...are little more than tree-wavings."

When he could no longer concentrate on his writing, John walked through the San Francisco Bay area. In some areas, he witnessed incredible new wealth. Squatters, many of whom were immigrants, lived in poverty near the waterfront. John liked to ramble east to climb Mount Diablo; other times he strolled north of San Francisco Bay through a grove of coastal redwoods, a species of sequoias.

Following a winter of writing, John decided to explore the sequoia region to learn about California's big trees. He intended to travel alone and on foot between Yosemite's Mariposa Grove and the Kaweah River region, about 200 miles (320 km) to the south. He would learn where the sequoias grew, how their root system worked, how the seeds reproduced—everything. He would take as long as he needed to find the answers.

John wandered 600 miles (970 km), going from tree to tree, from grove to grove. He visited lumber mills that produced millions of feet of lumber. On these and other trips, John was horrified when he encountered lumbermen felling sequoias, sometimes by dynamite. John could see no need to cut the giant trees because when they fell they shattered like glass, making much of the wood useless.

Back at the Swetts', John was often joined in the evenings by friends like John Swett and Joseph Le Conte, who gathered to talk in his room. They worried that most of the land in the West was privately owned by a few. Water sources, including natural reservoirs, were also privately owned; one corporation controlled the water supply for a large part of California. Speculators, mills, and public utility companies owned much of the best land.

During these sessions, William Keith encouraged John to send his writings to eastern magazines. Sometimes Keith taught him how to make his illustrations more natural looking. John's revised "Living Glaciers" was published in *Harper's Magazine*, which helped give him national recognition as a naturalist.

In January 1876, John prepared to give his first speech. He grew so anxious that he experienced nausea and chills. To help his friend, Keith put one of his Yosemite paintings on the stage. While peering at the landscape, John forgot his nervousness. He spoke clearly and forcefully about the mountains he knew and loved. But for the rest of his life, he struggled with pre-speech jitters.

A month after the speech, he published "God's First Temples—How Shall We Preserve Our Forests?" in a Sacramento newspaper. The theme—forest conservation—was inspired by his years of travel. He criticized the sheep owners for allowing overgrazing in the mountain pastures. For the first time, John publicly advocated laws to protect the wilderness, and voiced his growing concerns through the newspaper.

Since the Civil War, John had watched the West open up to exploration, settlement, and the rapid exploitation of its natural resources. New leaders were emerging—financiers and entrepreneurs—who advocated the making of money by using those resources. Fewer Americans lived according to the philosophical, nature-oriented words of Henry David Thoreau or Ralph Waldo Emerson.

Most city dwellers did not understand the natural beauty outside of town. Frustrated, John wrote, "Everybody needs beauty as well as bread, places to play in and pray in, where Nature may heal and cheer and give strength to body and soul alike."

After another winter of wandering around the West, he sailed down the San Joaquin and, shortly after it merges with the Sacramento River, docked his homemade boat at Martinez. From there he walked two miles (3 km) to the Alhambra Valley and John and Louisiana Strentzel's fruit ranch. His green coat was faded and worn, and his uncombed hair hung to his shoulders.

Years before, John Strentzel had invited the young Scotsman to visit his ranch. John Muir finally decided to call.

During the spring of 1878, John visited the ranch again and again, claiming he wanted to talk to Dr. Strentzel about horticulture, the cultivating of fruits. In reality, at the age of 40, shy, awkward John was courting the Strentzels' only daughter.

Louie—with dark hair and gray eyes—was a country girl by choice. At the age of 31, she preferred the quiet ranch life with her parents. Neighbors and friends asked her to make floral wreaths for funerals and provide flowers for weddings. Louie and her mother supported many charities, donating money to the churches and even giving land to the Methodist church and library in Martinez.

John Strentzel stands in front of his ranch near Martinez.

*Louie Wanda
Strentzel*

Louie and John walked through the orchards and talked. They explored the rolling hills and the lush valleys that encompassed the larger Alhambra Valley. Louie was interested in astronomy and, during evening strolls, shared her knowledge of the stars and constellations with John. Away from the ranch, John wrote to the Strentzels often. He began to write to Louie in 1879. John hinted in letters to his sisters and brothers that he was lonely and eager for his own home.

His quiet romance with Louie was observed by her parents and the ranch hands, but the couple never shared their feelings with friends. One evening in June 1879, Louie woke her mother and, overcome with emotion, said that she was engaged to John. Louisiana Strentzel recorded in her diary that "Mr. Muir is the only man that the Dr. [Strentzel] and I have ever felt that we could take into our family...and he is the only one that Louie has ever loved, altho' she has had many offers of marriage."

John told Louie he intended to go north to Puget Sound, perhaps as far as Alaska. When he returned—and he was not sure when—they would make wedding plans.

After seeing the Olympic Mountains, which stretched north into British Columbia and south into Oregon, John traveled north on a steamer. Alaska's wilderness lured him. He stopped first at Fort Wrangell, a Native American town with a large number of Presbyterian missionaries. John investigated the woods around the fort. He examined flowers he had never seen before and greeted other "flower muggins" he had known elsewhere.

John became a friend and hiking companion of S. Hall Young, a Presbyterian missionary. One day, as they were ascending a mountain peak, Young fell to a precipice, dislocating both shoulders. John lowered him 1,000 feet (3,000 m) to a glacier below. He reset one shoulder, then the other. By half-carrying Young, and building fires to warm him, John hauled the missionary to safety 24 hours later.

Several months passed. John and the now-healthy S. Hall Young traveled 800 miles (1,300 km) to Sitadaka Bay, which would later be called Glacier Bay. John became one of the first white people to see the bay, where he paddled among drifting icebergs and fjords, or inlets surrounded by steep cliffs. On land, he viewed and measured glaciers, named several, and walked upon one glacier that would later bear his name.

S. Hall Young stands atop Childs Glacier in 1910, top. *John Muir and other naturalists explore a glacier in Alaska,* bottom.

*Crevasses
run through
the top of
Muir Glacier.*

Glaciers push rocks and soil into ridges called moraines. This moraine stands beside Hidden Glacier in Alaska.

Later in 1880, John went on the Corwin expedition to Alaska, in search of the lost steamer Jeannette. This is his sketch of the first landing on Wrangel Island, located in the East Siberian Sea.

His guides were four Native Americans, led by Toyatte, "a grand old Stickeen nobleman" from the Stikine tribe. For the first time, John began to understand Native Americans, and recognized that their lives had been changed by the coming of European settlers who brought their religion and way of life. John named a glacier Toyatte in honor of the chief; the Stikines called John the "Ice Chief," an equally high tribute.

Late in November, John headed south and was reunited with Louie. As the rain poured down on April 14, 1880, John and Louie were married in the Strentzels' ranch house beneath a bower of apple blossoms. The day after the ceremony, John worked in the orchards and vineyards, determined to become a good horticulturist and breadwinner.

In one of the first letters written after his marriage, John wrote, "I am now the happiest man in the world."

John Muir stands in his vineyards. Behind him is the Victorian house that was built in 1881.

EIGHT

Farming and Mountain Climbing

1880-1892

Before the fall harvest, John sailed again for Alaska, the only area that he believed matched the Sierra Nevada in grandeur. He and Louie had agreed that he needed to go to the wilderness once a year. Louie had little interest in travel that involved camping out on Alaskan glaciers or in forests. She feared bears and mountain lions, and she disliked staying in primitive lodgings. Her world revolved around the ranch and her garden. She was interested in world affairs and especially enjoyed reading, so she cherished John's frequent letters and sketches.

John arrived in Fort Wrangell and met his friend S. Hall Young. For several months, John explored and measured glaciers. He traveled on foot or by canoe, often camping for days at a time. Stickeen, a little black dog, "unfussy as a tree," frequently trotted at his heel mile after mile. Once, when the rough, icy surface of a glacier began to slice Stickeen's feet and make them bleed, John wrapped the dog's paws with pieces of his handkerchief.

One wild, stormy morning John rose early to investigate Taylor Glacier, and Stickeen insisted upon going along. After a full day of exploration, John and Stickeen turned for home.

They found themselves confronted by a crevasse about 50 feet (15 m) wide. John realized that the only way across was a sliver of ice, several feet below where they stood, that bridged the expanse—perhaps 1,000 feet (300 m) deep.

The storm worsened, bringing blinding snow, as John axed steps in the ice down to the crossing. He straddled the thin bridge and inched across. When he reached the other side, he chipped another set of steps to climb up the nearly vertical face of the crevasse onto the surface of the glacier. Stickeen realized his predicament and started to whine, desperately seeking another way across. John coaxed him to work his careful way down the steps and across the sliver of a bridge. Then with a scramble, Stickeen flew up the cliff and past John to safety. By moonlight, man and dog joyfully leaped crevasses, climbed over boulders and tree branches on the moraines, and eventually returned to camp.

Stickeen stayed at John's side for the rest of the trip. When John returned to California, he left Stickeen with his master, S. Hall Young, and never saw the little dog again.

For the rest of his life, John repeated the story of Stickeen, the brave dog with the big heart. *Stickeen,* published in 1909 as a short book, became one of the most popular dog stories ever written.

Back home that autumn, John began to convert more of the 2,600 acres (1,050 hectares) of the Alhambra Valley ranch into vineyards or orchards. He grew good cash crops—Bartlett pears, Tokay grapes, and cherries. He planted the vines and saplings himself, or closely supervised the hired hands, many of whom were Chinese immigrants. Louie did the accounting and often gave ranch work to needy men with families.

John in his buggy became a familiar sight—a lean, whiskered man in work clothes, headed to the wharf or to the

Like her father, Annie Wanda Muir was lively, outgoing, and had a vivid imagination.

bank with a laundry bag of cash at his side. He studied the markets to find out what his crops were worth, and he drove a hard bargain.

On March 25, 1881, John and Louie's first child, Annie Wanda, was born. The entire household revolved around Wanda. John, who turned 43 that spring, wrote to his sister that "our own little big girl makes the home, and the farm, and the vineyard, and the hills, and the whole landscape far or near, shine for us."

About midday, Louie or Grandmother Strentzel often carried Wanda into the fields where John worked. He would pause from planting or pruning to play with his daughter or walk her along a creek or up a canyon. He taught Wanda the names of flowers as soon as she could talk.

It was a busy time. While living in temporary housing, Louisiana and John Strentzel were building their own home on the property. They had given their original house and some acreage to John and Louie. Over the years, John and Louie

The Muir-Strentzel ranch, with the Victorian house on the knoll to the left and the railroad tracks leading to San Francisco in the background

filled their home with books, artwork, and fine furniture—a contrast to John's childhood house in Wisconsin.

Before long, John's in-laws moved into their 16-room Victorian home, which was on a hilltop more than a mile away from the Muirs' house. All the rooms had high ceilings; many rooms also had brick and marble fireplaces.

At night John prepared government reports on Arctic botany and glaciation, based on specimens he had collected during an 1881 trip to the northern part of Alaska. During the day, he put in long, tedious hours on the ranch. Within a few years, he became quite wealthy. He grew thin and cranky because he disliked farming and yearned for his beloved mountains. At times he developed a hacking cough, and the profanity he had learned as a boy in Scotland resurfaced.

In 1884 John and Louie traveled by carriage to Yosemite, leaving Wanda in her grandmother's care. John wanted Louie to see Yosemite through his eyes; Louie wanted John to get away from the demands of ranch life. They toured the valley and nearby sites, but Louie was no mountaineer. Neither strayed far from the mail or telegraph office because they both worried about Wanda and the elderly Strentzels.

In a letter to Wanda, John sketched himself pushing Louie up a mountain in Yosemite.

After the short trip, John was back working long hours at the ranch. That fall he had a powerful premonition that his father was dying. Louie convinced him to go home. John boarded the transcontinental train.

Seven of the Muir children—their way paid by John— arrived in Kansas City where their father lived with Joanna, the youngest Muir. Daniel Muir lay on his deathbed. Except for Maggie, who was ill, all of the children were with their father when he died.

John visited his mother in Portage, Wisconsin, before returning to California. Shortly after John arrived home, a

When John found his sister Annie, below, *in ill health in Portage in 1885, he convinced her to come back with him to California. She stayed at the ranch for three years and regained her health.*

*Annie Wanda and
Helen Lillian Muir*

second daughter, Helen, was born on January 23, 1886. Frail and sickly due to respiratory problems, Helen's life hung by a thread. For a year and a half, John seldom left the ranch. Editors and friends begged him to write books and articles. John refused. His journals and nature notes lay untouched in his study.

In the summer of 1888, Louie persuaded John to get away, since Helen's health seemed to have improved. Louie encouraged him to renew his spirit in the wilderness and gather information for writing projects. John agreed.

He also agreed to contribute to, and edit, two volumes of nature studies about the Pacific Coast, to be called *Picturesque California*. William Keith would do some of the illustrations.

The two of them headed northwest with other friends on a fact-finding trip for *Picturesque California*. Near Mount Shasta, John witnessed the remains of once-beautiful forests now leveled for lumber. This single-minded "money-grubbing" shocked him.

John stands at the foot of a giant sugar pine.

Throughout Oregon and Washington, he saw similar forest devastation. It enraged him. How could anyone be so unthinking? John hoped that a few specimens of the sugar pine, his favorite tree, "might be spared to the world, not as dead lumber, but as living trees...set apart and protected for public use."

In Washington he scaled 14,410-foot (4,392-m)-high Mount Rainier as an afterthought, writing Louie, "Did not mean to climb it, but got excited, and soon was on top." Due to John's influence, Mount Rainier National Park was created a decade later in 1899.

Louie wrote to him from home. "A ranch that needs and takes the sacrifice of a noble life, or work, ought to be flung away.... The Alaska book and the Yosemite book, dear John, must be written."

At the ranch in Martinez, they talked. Louie wanted the man she had married eight years before, a writer and a naturalist who loved to explore the wilderness, not an unhappy, unhealthy, restive farmer. Louie, a shrewd businesswoman, knew they could afford to sell and lease large portions of the land over the next few years. As a result of John's hard work on the ranch, he and Louie were financially secure.

Once again, John took up his pen and his passion for nature. He delved into the dusty manuscripts and notes cluttering his office. He answered letters from editors who wanted his ideas and articles. Gazing out the window of his "scribble den," he thought seriously about writing books, or "book making" as he called it.

In June 1889, Robert Underwood Johnson, the New York editor for *Century* and an outdoorsman and poet, came west to convince John to contribute to his magazine. Johnson believed strongly in changing things for the better through the written word.

John decided to take the eastern-based editor on a pack trip to Yosemite a few days later. John could not contain his excitement over rediscovering Yosemite after a five-year absence. Like a child, he shared every detail with Johnson. They talked nonstop around the campfire at night.

John was heartsick at the changes he witnessed. Trees were cut down; hayfields and corrals dotted the valley. Sheep and cattle, or "hoofed locusts" as John called them, overgrazed the meadows. "The Valley looked like a frowsy, backwoods pasture," he told Johnson. Lincoln's 1864 Act did not protect the higher mountain meadows or the headwaters of streams that coursed into Yosemite. Something needed to be done.

That June night, the two men decided to team up and work to make the Yosemite area into a national park. Besides giving speeches, John would write for *Century*—portraying the wonders of the area, outlining the proposed boundaries, and asking the people to help make it happen. Back home in the East, Johnson would seek to have a bill introduced in Congress, using his numerous government connections. The two friends knew a Yosemite park was possible. Yellowstone had become a national park in 1872; in 1885 part of the Adirondack Mountains had become a national park.

The intense emotion of fighting to protect his beloved Yosemite affected John's well-being. Suffering from stomach problems and a cough, he decided to go to Alaska after completing his articles for *Century*. He cobbled his shoes with thick soles and made a sleeping bag out of bearskin, red wool, and a canvas sheet. From Alaska he wrote to Wanda of sleeping like a caterpillar in a cocoon. Before long, John regained his "wilderness health."

In August and September of 1890, John's articles, "Treasures of the Yosemite" and "Features of the Proposed Yosemite National Park," appeared in *Century*. More than 200,000 subscribers learned of the devastation John had seen with Robert Underwood Johnson a few months before.

Back home in late September, John learned that his articles had been reprinted by newspapers across the nation.

Everyone was talking, but not everyone agreed with John's ideas. One politician wrote that John Muir and *Century* wanted to cheat California of its natural resources, and claimed that Muir had cut trees in Yosemite Valley like any other lumberman.

John's only rebuttal appeared in a local newspaper, the *Oakland Tribune*. "I was employed...to saw lumber from fallen timber...I never cut down a single tree in the Yosemite, nor sawed a tree cut down by any other person there."

After reading the *Century* articles, Secretary of the Interior John Noble stepped in. Already a fan of John Muir's writing, Noble emphasized the importance of preserving America's wilderness to President Benjamin Harrison.

The Yosemite National Park bill was introduced in Congress and became law on October 1, 1890, preserving approximately 1,200 square miles (3,100 square km). Sequoia and General Grant National Parks in the southern Sierra Nevada were also created in 1890 to protect large stands of sequoia trees. California still retained control of Yosemite Valley and Mariposa Grove.

John dreamed of expanding the boundary of Sequoia Park, but family matters commanded his attention. Dr. Strentzel had died, so John and Louie moved into the big Victorian house to provide companionship and care for frail Mrs. Strentzel. The close-knit family mourned Dr. Strentzel's death, especially Wanda and Helen, who missed their beloved grandfather. John found little time to fight for his causes. The report concerning Sequoia Park's expansion failed in the congressional committee.

The following spring, John's sister Margaret and her husband, John Reid, arrived to take charge of the ranch work. A year later, John's brother David and his second wife,

Wanda and Helen

Juliette, also moved to Martinez. This delighted John, because for years he had begged his family to join him in California and enjoy the plentiful food and mild climate. Often Helen and Wanda, sometimes accompanied by "Papa," walked to Aunt Margaret's house to visit. They also called on Uncle David and his family. Sometimes Aunt Margaret and Aunt Sarah—now widowed and visiting California—came to the Muir house for a dress-fitting or to socialize.

At the age of 53, John was finally free of ranching responsibilities. He joined a network of hikers and university members in the San Francisco Bay area. They wanted to create a club with several goals: to enjoy the out-of-doors, to appreciate nature, and most importantly to preserve the wilderness. John believed he could best achieve his dreams by uniting people with common goals. He liked the idea of the club.

John knew that outdoor-oriented clubs—such as the Appalachian Mountain Club—were springing up in the East. The Audubon Society had organized in the 1880s. It was time to create a western-based club to protect the new national parks. The first meeting took place in May 1892. By June 4, the organization had a name: Sierra Club. Twenty-seven men joined and unanimously elected John Muir president, a position he held until his death.

John returned home to celebrate that evening. A dinner guest recalled that "I venture to say it was the happiest day of his life.... He was hilarious with joy!"

John enjoyed Sierra Club outings from the club's beginning through the rest of his life. Here he poses with a Sierra Club group on the trail to Hetch Hetchy in 1909.

John at work in his "scribble den"

NINE

A Proud Papa

1892-1898

John wrote at his desk, puffing on his long, thistle-stem pipe. "The Oaks" by William Keith hung over the mantel. Untidy stacks of manuscripts, books, and sketches cluttered the floor. Using an eagle's quill dipped in a bottle of ink, John edited *Picturesque California*, wrote letters, and revised his notes and sketches.

For the first year of its existence, the Sierra Club had its work cut out as guardian of the Sierra Nevada. A group of loggers and sheep and cattle ranchers supported a congressional bill to eliminate half of Yosemite National Park. Under John's presidency, club members swung into action by writing letters, speaking to members of Congress, and sending telegrams. As a result, the bill was narrowly defeated. This victory started the Sierra Club on its path to becoming one of the most powerful conservation organizations in the world.

John, who was seldom humble, enjoyed his new Sierra Club role and his growing national prestige as a leader of land preservation battles. He let Louie trim his hair and beard. She selected tailored suits for him. John continued to pin a sprig of greenery to his lapel.

Friends flocked to the ranch. Some stayed for days, others just came for a meal. Guests enjoyed picnics—with Louie's homemade bread, baked beans, chicken, and freshly

*The Muirs sit on the front porch of their business manager—
the son-in-law of John's sister Margaret.*

picked fruit—in the garden or in various scenic spots in the
Alhambra Valley area. At dinner John spoke of meeting grizzly
bears, of finding new flowers, and of exploring the Sierra
Nevada, which he called the "Range of Light." Spellbound
guests listened. Louie, a charming and gracious hostess, preferred to stay in the background.

Helen and Wanda were not as quiet. Every night they
eagerly demanded that their father tell another installment

of Paddy Grogan's adventures—an original tale John had concocted about an Irish boy and his kangaroo "horse." The adventures of Paddy Grogan were never written down, and friends said that the world lost a great children's story.

William Keith visited frequently. Day and night, the two friends bantered back and forth in their Scottish dialect. They recited Robert Burns's poetry to Helen and Wanda and led the sisters on hilarious romps in the hills surrounding the ranch. Botany lessons were part of every walk, for John wanted his "bairns" to love plants, animals, and people. "More wide knowledge, less arithmetic and grammar, keeps the heart alive." John named one hill in the Alhambra Valley Mount Wanda; another he called Mount Helen.

"Johnnie" and "Willie" played pranks and games that often included Wanda and Helen. There were many hiding places in the big house and a treasure-filled attic to explore on rainy days. As Wanda recalled, "Father was the biggest jolliest child of us all."

However, John became a dour, difficult Scotsman when he was writing, for "pen work" never came easily to him. He demanded quiet. His daughters practiced their violins and the piano in a soundproof, brick-walled practice room above the kitchen and tiptoed around the house when their father worked in his "scribble den." He kept in touch with the world by mail, not the telephone, because he disliked shouting into the new-fangled gadget.

But John could seldom stay home for long. In May 1893, he set off for the East Coast and Europe. He met his editor and friend, Robert Underwood Johnson, in New England, and they toured the homes and graves of Ralph Waldo Emerson and Henry David Thoreau. John walked to Walden Pond, where Thoreau had lived part of his solitary, reflective life.

John attended a whirlwind of parties where everyone wanted to meet him. His reputation combined with his looks—weathered face, beard, bright blue eyes, and rich voice—made John a living legend. He told the story of Stickeen over and over again. Even the servants listened behind half-closed doors. He wrote Louie that "I had no idea I was so well known."

Robert Underwood Johnson introduced John to dozens of celebrities. He met writers Sarah Orne Jewett, Rudyard Kipling, and Samuel Langhorne Clemens—also known as Mark Twain. Some of the people he met became longtime friends, such as Charles Sargent, a Harvard botanist, and John Burroughs, a famous bird and nature essayist from New England. The two Johns had previously admired each other from a distance. Although opposites in temperament, they both had a keen sense of humor, enjoyed a good argument, and loved solitude.

In 1899 the "two Johnnies," Burroughs and Muir, went on the Harriman expedition to Alaska. Burroughs went along as the historian. The other members of the expedition were scientists.

*Dunbar, Scotland
in 1893*

John sailed to Scotland and rode to Dunbar, where he rambled through the countryside and relived his childhood memories. He saw England, then Switzerland, circling back to Dunbar. Noticing the poverty around him, he arranged to give some money to the poor of Dunbar, which he did every Christmas until his death.

Returning to the United States, John received a telegram from Louie urging him to travel to Washington, D.C. Taking her advice, he called upon the secretary of the interior and other government officials. Seldom shy or at a loss for words, John pushed conservation to anyone who would listen.

The grape harvest was underway when John returned to Martinez in the fall of 1893. He forced himself to get busy with "book making." He revised and edited his early essays, such as those on the water ouzel and the Douglas squirrel. After he added six new chapters, his first book, *The Mountains of California*, took shape. He took his editor's advice and tried to eliminate unnecessary adjectives—especially his favorites, "grand" and "glorious." Louie reviewed everything first, for John submitted nothing without her approval.

The Mountains of California was published in 1894 and has become a classic. In addition to recounting John's life in the mountains, the book reflects his philosophy that America's forests must be saved as national parks and reserves.

Timber and mining organizations, who feared land preservation, opposed the ideas in *The Mountains of California*. But the book became an immediate success among conservationists. Pleased by the positive response, John said, "I am trying to write another book, but it is harder than mountaineering."

John continued to enjoy spending time with his daughters, for he realized how quickly they were growing up. Wanda, like her mother, was calm and quiet. Helen had inherited her father's imagination and outgoing spirit. A proud "Papa," he wrote about their childhood in his journal. On Helen's 9th birthday, he recorded: "She celebrated the day on the hills. She climbs well & is in perfect health. An unspeakable blessing after the extreme delicacy of her earliest years." On Wanda's 14th birthday, he wrote: "Happy girl...I dread pain & trouble in so sweet & good a life.—If only death and pain could be abolished."

One day in June 1896 at the ranch, John had a premonition that he must go east if he wanted to see his mother again.

He took the train to Wisconsin, gathering relatives along the way. In Portage, Sarah rushed out of the house, exclaiming, "Oh, John, surely God has sent you. Mother is terribly ill!" Anne Muir, who was now 83, revived from her deathbed to visit with her children. Feeling she was out of immediate danger, John traveled to Harvard to receive an honorary degree. During that time, Anne died peacefully.

Instead of heading home, John joined the Forestry Commission as a guide and an advisor. John Muir, Charles Sargent, Gifford Pinchot, and other "good forest fellows" planned to travel west to inspect the forests on public land and report back to President Grover Cleveland.

Everywhere they went, the Forestry Commission saw the results of the misuses of government land: illegal mining operations, hills denuded of trees, and exposed soil due to overgrazing. John wrote Louie that "wherever the white man goes, the groves vanish." In contrast, his frequent letters to Wanda and Helen were full of entertaining stories with little sketches on the margins.

The members of the Forestry Commission met to prepare their findings. John believed that a system of forest management was needed immediately. Some, including Gifford Pinchot, advocated a different approach. The members compromised and reported back to President Cleveland that the forests should be safeguarded by the military until professional foresters could get organized.

On the 165th anniversary of George Washington's birthday, President Cleveland signed a bill to protect 21,000,000 acres (8,500,000 hectares) of forest, all in the West. To Cleveland's surprise, he created a national fury. Loggers, miners, and those in related industries worried about losing their jobs. By the 1880s, the great eastern forests had been logged out.

Commercial loggers were depending on the western forests. The lumber, stock, and mining companies threatened unsuccessfully to impeach the outgoing president.

Because of the national outcry protesting the preservation of western forests, Congress passed a compromise bill to suspend their creation until 1898. The new president, William McKinley, signed the compromise bill into law, in effect canceling the Forestry Commission's report.

A lumberjack sits on a felled tree in Merced County.

John stands at the foot of a sequoia.

John angrily put aside his other work to write for the *Atlantic Monthly,* a popular magazine supporting conservation. "The American Forests" was his supreme effort to save the trees.

> The forests of America, however slighted by man, must have been a great delight to God; for they were the best he ever planted...

> Any fool can destroy trees. They cannot run away;
> and if they could they would still be destroyed, —chased
> and hunted down as long as fun or a dollar could be
> got out of their bark hides, branching horns, or mag-
> nificent bole backbones [tree trunks]... Through all
> the wonderful, eventful centuries since Christ's time—
> and long before that—God has cared for these trees
> ...but he cannot save them from fools, —only Uncle
> Sam can do that.

John wanted the government to protect its public forests against what he called the "invading of destroyers." He also believed in saving the forests for their spiritual value, point-ing out that "thousands of tired, nerve-shaken, over-civilized people are beginning to find out that going to the mountains is going home; that wildness is a necessity."

In between his writing, John took several trips, including another fact-finding mission to Alaska in 1897. He arrived during the Klondike Gold Rush. He wired news of the gold rush to the Hearst newspaper chain, describing the frenzied attitude of the miners and the calm trees peering down upon them.

When John reached home, Mrs. Strentzel was near death. She died two weeks later. John missed her and retreated into his "scribble den" to work.

His second *Atlantic Monthly* article, "Wild Parks and Forest Reservations of the West," came out in January 1898. His essay pointedly criticized the policies of Gifford Pinchot, who had become a prominent government forester.

Pinchot was well aware of the economic value of land in the West. He believed in the regulated use of public land for lumbering, mining, and grazing. John disagreed. He insisted that wilderness land be preserved in its natural state not only for its beauty, but because of its unique position in the

John returned to his "scribble den" to save his beloved trees.

environment. He sensed that tourism was the key to preserving the land. Gradually, because of their very different philosophies, the gap widened between the two men.

John stands with Theodore Roosevelt and his party at the foot of the Grizzly Giant in Mariposa Grove in 1903.

TEN

Crusading for the Wilderness

1898-1906

In the fall of 1898, John wrote to Louie, "Dear Lassie, it is settled that I go on a short visit to Florida with Sargent." By carriage and on foot, John retraced some of his steps on his 1,000-mile (1,600-km) trip to Florida. Now 59, John wanted to salute "the grand, godly, round-headed trees of the east side of America that I learned to love and beneath which I used to weep with joy when nobody knew me."

The following year, John was invited by E. H. Harriman, president of the Southern Pacific Railroad, to join an expedition of 23 scientists who would explore the coast of Alaska. Sparing no expense, Harriman had outfitted a steamer ship with science labs and a large social hall where the scientists could talk about their discoveries during the 10-week-long trip.

John made new friends wherever he went. This, his seventh trip to Alaska, was no different. Before long, expedition members Henry Gannett, chief geographer of the U.S. Geological Survey, and Dr. C. Hart Merriam, chief of the U.S. Biological Survey, visited John and his family at the Martinez ranch.

At the end of 1899, Wanda decided that she wanted to go to college. John disapproved of college for his daughters, believing that they should remain home until they married. During their childhood, he had encouraged informal studies directed by a series of governesses. But, forgetting his own rich experiences at the University of Wisconsin, he apparently was not ready to believe that his "bairns" were young adults.

Wanda seldom opposed her father. But this time she packed her trunks and, with her mother's blessings, took the train to Berkeley. She studied in a private girls' school to polish her skills and, in January 1901, enrolled at the University of California. She sent bubbling letters home to "Dear Mama" about her interests in music, cultural activities, and her sorority—Gamma Phi Delta. It took John several months to accept that his daughter "was as unstoppable as an avalanche."

Later in 1901, John took Wanda and Helen to Yosemite on the Sierra Club's first organized outing. About one-third of the members were women. They were told to wear short

Wanda, left, *Helen, and John Muir on a Sierra Club trip to King's Canyon*

C. Hart Merriam, left, Wanda and Helen on horseback, and John, far right, *in Sequoia National Park*

skirts, no more than halfway between the knee and ankle, with bloomers underneath. Both Muir girls were accomplished horsewomen, and rode in divided skirts. John wore a suit, with his bow tie hidden under his beard and his pockets full of plant specimens.

The group made a base camp at Tuolumne Meadows, and John wrote Louie that "Wanda and Helen take to this life in the rocks and woods like ducks to water." The girls thought nothing of walking 25 to 30 miles (40 to 48 km) a day.

The girls and their father joined other Sierra Club trips, even traveling south to King's Canyon. They took up back-packing. Sometimes John was the leader and gave campfire talks at night. Caught up in his storytelling, he often forgot to eat. Wanda or Helen slipped him bits of food that he swallowed unknowingly. John especially liked camping with his daughters and other families, and he believed that people would resist the destruction of the places they had visited.

That September President William McKinley was assassinated. Vice President Theodore Roosevelt, an avid outdoors-man and an amateur naturalist, assumed the highest office in the land. When Roosevelt first addressed Congress in December 1901, he said that "the forest and water problems are perhaps the most vital internal questions of the United States at the present time." He wanted to learn about the forests and how to conserve natural resources. He also wanted to hear from John Muir.

John wrote immediately, surprised at becoming an advisor to the president. It surprised him even more when he received a letter from Roosevelt, who was planning to visit the West and wanted John to guide him through Yosemite. "My dear Mr. Muir," the letter began, "I do not want anyone with me but you, and I want to drop politics absolutely for four days and just be out in the open with you."

In May 1903, Theodore Roosevelt and John Muir traveled to Yosemite. The only other members of the group, two rangers and a cook, stayed in the background. The first night, they camped in Mariposa Grove near a cool spring. John and Roosevelt cooked steaks and drank coffee as they relaxed beneath the canopy of ancient sequoias.

Roosevelt and John stand on Overhanging Rock at Glacier Point. To the left of Roosevelt are Yosemite Falls.

At sunrise the following morning, the two men rode on horseback to Glacier Point, 3,214 feet (980 m) above Yosemite Valley. John delighted in watching the president's almost child-like enthusiasm over the breathtaking scenery—the mountains of the Sierra Nevada, endless forests, waterfalls plunging to the valley below, and the clear blue sky touching it all. Many times during the trip, the president whistled to the birds and they answered him.

They camped at the edge of a meadow the second night. After darkness descended, John made them mattresses of ferns, flowers, and cedar boughs. Before sleeping beneath blankets, they chatted about everything, for both were famous for their talkativeness. The president knew his birds; John spoke of flowers, rocks, and the forest.

John later told a friend that "I stuffed him pretty well regarding the timber thieves, and the destructive work of the lumbermen, and other spoilers of the forest." John probably urged Roosevelt to put the Yosemite Valley under federal control. Roosevelt, who thought of the mountains and prairies primarily as hunting preserves, listened to John talk of the critical need to protect the land.

They awoke the second morning to find themselves covered with four inches (10 cm) of snow. "I wouldn't miss this for anything," shouted Roosevelt. "This is bully! Hurrah for Yosemite!"

The president deliberately stayed away from the huge crowds who hoped to glimpse the famous figure in khaki, army hat, and bandanna. He also avoided an extravagant banquet and fireworks show planned in his honor. For his last night at Yosemite, President Roosevelt chose to camp in Bridalveil Meadow about 1½ miles (2½ km) from El Capitan, a massive rock rising 4,000 feet (1,200 m) above the valley floor. He enjoyed the sunset reflecting on the granite walls, as did John, who never tired of the changing colors in the valley.

The next morning, they parted as friends. Both knew that this short trip would have far-reaching results for conservation. The president confirmed that feeling when he spoke in Sacramento: "We are not building this country of ours for a day. It is to last through the ages."

During his presidency, Roosevelt tripled the square miles of national forests and doubled the number of national parks. By proclamation, he created 23 national monuments.

A few weeks after the presidential camping trip, John began a year-long, globe-trotting trip with Charles Sargent. As usual, Louie stayed at the ranch. After a whirlwind tour of Europe's cities and museums, the two men crossed into Russia. John wanted to see the great Russian forests of spruce, silver birch, and pines, interspersed with glacial lakes.

Suffering from acute food poisoning, he was carried on a stretcher to a train headed for the Black Sea and Caucasus Mountains. From the train, he saw vast forests of birch and larch trees.

Still sick and losing weight rapidly, John decided to leave Sargent and head alone to India and the 30,000-foot (9,000-m)-high Himalayas. He wanted to see deodar trees— large East Indian cedars. The brisk mountain air and the sight of the huge trees reminded him of California's redwoods. His health returned.

"There are a few more places I should see before I die," he wrote Louie. Next he traveled to Egypt and the Pyramids, and wondered what it would be like to scale the huge structures. He filled his journals with notes and sketches, and wrote detailed letters to Louie and the girls.

As a pampered guest on one of E. H. Harriman's steamers, he sailed to Australia and New Zealand. In Australia, he blissfully explored several forests, unaware that Helen was gravely ill with the first of many pneumonia attacks. He gathered botanical specimens and dried them in the sun on the ship's deck. He toured the Philippines, China, and Japan, giving botany lessons on the way.

When he arrived home a year later, he looked healthy and tan. His bags burst with plants and gifts for his family. Helen, now recovered from pneumonia, and Wanda greeted him at the dock in San Francisco.

John spent the next few months planning for California's 1905 legislature. A bill would be introduced to return Yosemite Valley to the federal government.

Wanda, Helen, Louie, and John Muir on the porch of the Victorian house

John believed strongly that California had mismanaged the Yosemite Valley. So did many other Californians. They had read and loved his 1901 book, *Our National Parks*, a collection of essays. Everyday citizens agreed with his philosophy of wilderness preservation, as did the Sierra Club and its secretary, William Colby.

John Muir and William Colby spoke before the legislature in Sacramento nine times. With the support of several California groups, especially the powerful influence of railroad magnate E. H. Harriman, the 1905 bill passed, making the valley part of Yosemite National Park.

That spring, Helen was often sick. Her doctor recommended that she live in the dry desert air for a year to regain her health. Wanda was a few months away from graduation when the family insisted upon her help. She dropped out of the university, leaving behind a suitor, Tom Hanna.

Always a homebody, Louie stayed home to oversee the ranch. Her own health was poor. She probably suffered from kidney problems, which made her figure and face puffy-looking. The two sisters and their father left for Arizona. They stayed in a large, rambling hotel at Adamana. John was optimistic that Helen would recover because he had "never breathed air more distinctly, palpably good."

They had only been there a few weeks when a telegram arrived. Louie had pneumonia. John, Helen, and Wanda rushed back to California. Apparently, Louie also had inoperable lung cancer. Helen could only stay a few days due to her own recurring health problems. She bid a tearful good-bye to her mother, knowing she would never see her again. About a month later, on August 6, 1905, Louie died and was buried in the family plot on the ranch.

Wanda and John returned to Arizona to be with Helen. For the first few months, John walked in a daze or spent long hours sleeping. He missed Louie. His solid, steady helpmate and confidant for 25 years, who had encouraged his creative freedom, was gone. Tributes poured in from friends such as C. Hart Merriam, who wrote that Louie "was a clever and noble woman, but so retiring that she was known only to a few."

From his hotel room, John listened to the endless desert winds. Sometimes he stared out his window. He began to notice the play of light on the yellow sand. He took brief hikes on the mesas. Within months, the naturalist in him resurfaced and he started to explore the Arizona desert.

On an outing with his daughters, John discovered a forest of wood that had become petrified, or turned into stone. The

John examines a petrified log with a magnifying lens. The presence of these logs in the desert means that there was once enough water to nourish large trees.

blue petrified wood stumps and logs fascinated him. So did the evidence of ancient Indian life—their pottery, their dwellings, and their rock drawings. He grew curious about desert plants. He wanted to know more about snakes and other desert inhabitants.

Helen pitched a tent near the hotel and slept outside. Day by day, her lungs healed in the warm, dry air. She grew strong enough to go horseback riding.

With Helen's health mending, John and Wanda returned to the ranch. Louie's spirit filled every corner of the house. John allowed nothing to be touched. Dust settled over everything, including the "scribble den" where a dozen book projects waited. A Chinese servant, Ah Fong, looked after the house.

Wanda rekindled her romance with Tom Hanna, an engineering student from the University of California. They became engaged.

John's only writing efforts consisted of letters to friends involved in the never-ending struggle to save the wilderness. For long hours at a time, he researched petrified forests in the library at the University of California at Berkeley. His thoughts focused on the stone trees in an area he called the "Blue Forest"—now Blue Mesa. With Helen and Wanda, John had watched tourists haul away the petrified logs for

Helen and Wanda, both wearing glasses, picnic with a group of friends in the petrified forest in 1906.

souvenirs. In Adamana, a mill crushed the logs to make an abrasive. Not one to keep silent, John brought this to public attention.

As a result of John's efforts, President Roosevelt created the Petrified Forest National Monument in December 1906. Arizona's Blue Forest and Black Forest were added later. That same year, the president set aside a portion of the Grand Canyon as a national monument. Under President Woodrow Wilson, the Grand Canyon officially became a national park in 1919.

In June Wanda married her college sweetheart. Tom and Wanda Hanna moved into the old adobe house below the big Victorian house on the ranch. Helen wrote that she would be

Tom and Wanda Hanna at home

John in Palm Springs, California, on his way to Arizona in 1905

well enough to come home in a few months. John's grief over Louie's death lessened as he looked forward to having both his "bairns" near him. He began to think about "book making" and fights ahead to save the wilderness.

John and Helen play with Stickeen at home in Martinez.

ELEVEN

The Fight Continues

1906-1914

Helen came home in August, seemingly in good health. For the next year and a half, father and daughter formed a team. Helen learned to type and helped her father with his writing projects. Every afternoon they hiked around the ranch, followed by Stickeen, a shepherd dog named in honor of the original dog. They often visited Wanda and Tom.

John encouraged Helen in all her interests, especially her love of trains. After befriending the local trainmen with fresh garden produce and homemade pies, the two often hopped the Santa Fe train that ran near their home. Helen knew all the engine numbers by heart and even recognized the various whistles. As a teenager, she had recorded train information in her diary and decorated her bedroom with train posters. Helen and John climbed in the cab for short rides, and Helen learned to operate the engine.

Because the big, empty, Victorian house seemed "under-peopled," they often invited friends to the ranch. On cool evenings, guests gathered around the open fire in the parlor. Candles and kerosene lamps provided the only light, for John deplored the newest invention—electricity. At dinner, John told captivating stories or gently teased Helen.

In the fall of 1907, John and William Keith—both nearly 70 years old—visited the Sierra Nevada. The Tuolumne River

John Muir and William Keith camp in a redwood grove on their way to Hetch Hetchy in 1907.

rushed by their campsite in the Hetch Hetchy Valley, a smaller version of Yosemite Valley with domes, granite cliffs, and waterfalls. When John had first explored the area as a young man, he had learned that the words Hetch Hetchy mean "a grass with edible seeds" in Miwok Indian language.

John worried about the future of the valley. Although Hetch Hetchy lay within a national park, the city of San Francisco had been eyeing the area for a cheap, reliable source of water and water power. Officials wanted to dam the Tuolumne River at the mouth of the deep-walled valley and pipe the water to San Francisco.

*John Muir and
John Burroughs
look over the
Grand Canyon
in 1909.
They shared
"a battling
friendship."*

San Francisco was water-conscious mainly as a result of the 1906 earthquake. After the rumbling had stopped, the city had burned for three days because most of the water lines had broken.

John also knew that in 1901 a federal bill had been passed authorizing the secretary of the interior to grant rights of way through national parks for artificial waterways—canals, pipelines, aqueducts, dammed rivers—as long as they did not interfere with public interests. John believed that the development of Hetch Hetchy would signal that no public park would ever be safe from similar commercialization.

When he returned home from his trip with William Keith, John found Helen seriously ill again with pneumonia. Her doctor recommended two years of desert air to mend her damaged lungs. John built his daughter a cabin in the Mojave Desert near Daggett, California, before returning to Martinez.

Although John did not like politics, he again used his influence to try to save Hetch Hetchy, predicting that "this Yosemite fight promises to be the 'worst ever.'" He refused to let constant colds and headaches interfere with his work.

Gifford Pinchot, now the country's chief forester, led the opposition in Washington. President Roosevelt supported Pinchot and believed that the reservoir from the dammed river would cause no serious harm to the Sierra Nevada. Disappointed with the president's stand, John vowed to continue the battle because "we must be true to ourselves."

In his free time, he traveled back and forth from Daggett to Martinez, taking occasional trips to the mountains. He went on an outing to Yosemite with naturalist John Burroughs. Another time, John joined a Sierra Club outing of 220 men and women and gave them impromptu and instructive talks. His blue eyes sparkled and his hands cut through the air as he accentuated points in his stories. These diversions helped him forget his burdens and he became his old, rollicking self.

In October 1909, he met the new president, William Howard Taft, in Yosemite. Unlike President Roosevelt, President Taft was followed by guards and hoards of reporters. The president, who weighed more than 300 pounds (140 kilograms), was too large to ride a horse. The two men traveled by stagecoach to the different scenic spots in Yosemite.

John showed the president maps and charts that he had prepared, outlining future plans for the park. He proposed to link the Yosemite Valley, Tuolumne Meadows, Tuolumne Canyon, and the Hetch Hetchy Valley with a system of roads and trails. John knew that tourism was the key to protecting Yosemite in its natural state.

Although not an outdoorsman, President Taft decided to hike four miles (6 km) from Glacier Point to the valley floor.

John accompanied him, talking nonstop about the evils of destroying Hetch Hetchy. The rest of Taft's staff followed on horses and mules.

At times, the 71-year-old naturalist resembled an evangelistic preacher, much like his father. Taft, who had a great sense of humor, teased John as they hiked and commented that the Yosemite Valley floor would make a nice farm. Despite his bantering, President Taft was impressed by John Muir and opposed the damming of Hetch Hetchy during his presidency.

It was a difficult period for John. In the San Francisco area, some Sierra Club members believed that damming Hetch Hetchy offered the best, most inexpensive solution to the

President Taft and his party stop in front of the Wawona Tunnel Tree in Mariposa Grove.

city's water problems. Disappointed with the opposition, John thought about resigning from the Sierra Club.

Instead, taking the advice of Sierra Club secretary William Colby, he and other interested club members formed the Society for the Preservation of the National Parks, with John Muir as president. John continued to try to convince Congress and various government officials to save the valley.

During the years of the Hetch Hetchy battle, John worked harder than ever on his books, starting with his autobiography. He had at least a dozen projects in mind but wrote slowly because, as he once told a visitor, he would be ashamed to send out a careless piece of work.

In 1911, John published *My First Summer in the Sierra*, taken from his original journals. Two years later, he bundled up his other Yosemite notes and published these as *The Yosemite*, a guidebook to the region. He sorted his extensive notes on Alaska and began another book.

John published *The Story of My Boyhood and Youth* in 1913. Many readers, including old friends, were shocked by his harsh childhood in Scotland and Wisconsin. John's youngest sister, Joanna, wrote, "The portion relating to yourself and the family was read in tears, and I wished with all my heart it had not been so true."

Every winter, John spent some time in southern California—writing, staying with old friends, and avoiding the damp, foggy Martinez weather. When his well-meaning friends honored him with too many formal dinners and receptions, he packed his worn satchel and went to Daggett. Helen had married Buel Funk, a cattle rancher, and now lived permanently in the desert where her health remained stable.

William Keith died in the spring of 1911, leaving John without his closest friend. A few weeks later, John announced that he would visit South America. Friends tried to discourage him, but John had dreamed of visiting the Amazon River since his walk to Florida 50 years earlier. "The world's big and I want to have a good look at it before it gets dark."

He sailed 1,000 miles (1,600 km) up the Amazon, reveling in the thick jungle vegetation. When he arrived in Buenos Aires, Argentina, John was besieged by scientists and reporters who wanted to meet the famous naturalist. Surprised that his fame had spread so far, he told his interviewers he was studying the trees of South America.

Crossing into Chile, John rode hundreds of miles by buggy and then horseback. On the western slopes of the Andes Mountains, he saw monkey-puzzle trees—strange, grotesque trees covered with prickly needles that kept out the monkeys. That night the 74-year-old "tramp," as he called himself, slept under the stars near the ancient trees.

Feeling healthy and adventurous, he took a steamer to Africa instead of coming home as planned. He arrived in Cape Town, South Africa. From there he took a train north to Victoria Falls to see baobab trees, known for their skin-like bark and massive trunks and branches. A child led him to a baobab grove about a mile from Victoria Falls. John wrote home about "one of the greatest of the great tree days of my lucky life." He filled notebooks with sketches of the trees and the mountainous countryside.

After a seven-month-long trip, he returned to the United States. He celebrated his 75th birthday on April 21st in New England with John Burroughs and then hurried home. He could not wait to see Wanda and Helen and his grandsons.

Although the old house seemed dusty and was filled with memories of Louie, John set to work on *Travels in Alaska*. Never fond of "book making," he needed little excuse to put down his pen and play with Wanda and Tom's sons: Strentzel, John, and Richard. They romped in the gardens for hours and met the "flower muggins" on the hills surrounding the ranch house. He also visited Helen, Buel, and their two sons— Muir and Stanley—in Daggett.

He traveled to Yosemite in October 1913 for a national parks conference. Officials were discussing park problems and solutions, such as whether or not to allow cars in the park. John later said, "under certain precautionary restrictions, these useful, progressive, blunt-nosed mechanical beetles will hereafter be allowed to puff their way into all the parks and mingle their gas-breath with the breath of the pines and waterfalls." Cars were permitted on Yosemite roads in 1913.

John plays with his Hanna grandsons— Strentzel, John, and Richard.

At the age of 75, John continued to enjoy walking. Every day, he strolled to the nearby ranch of his long-time friend, John Swett. The two white-haired men rocked on the front porch and argued about education, recalled family camping trips to Yosemite, and talked about the upcoming presidential election. John voted for William Howard Taft, but Woodrow Wilson became the new president.

The following May, the two Johns received honorary degrees from the University of California. The college honored John Swett as the founder of California's public school system. John Muir's citation read,

> John Muir, Born in Scotland, reared in the University of Wisconsin, by final choice a Californian, Widely travelled Observer of the world we dwell in, Man of Science and of Letters, Friend and Protector of Nature, Uniquely gifted to Interpret unto others Her mind and ways.

A few months later, John Swett died unexpectedly, just as the Hetch Hetchy campaign shifted into full swing. Although John had many friends supporting his cause, many others, including Jeanne Carr, were gone. To lessen his sorrow, he plunged into the fight, firing off letters, telegrams, and newspaper articles. In one appeal he wrote, "These temple destroyers ...seem to have a perfect contempt for Nature, and instead of lifting their eyes to the God of the Mountains, lift them to the Almighty Dollar." To a friend, John wrote, "This is the twenty-third year of almost continual battle for preservation of Yosemite National Park, sadly interrupting my natural work."

The bill—called the Raker Act—to allow San Francisco to use Hetch Hetchy as a reservoir inched through Congress. John wrote to Helen that "I'll be relieved when it's settled, for it's killing me."

The bill passed in the Senate and on December 19, 1913, President Wilson signed the Raker Act into law. Sick with exhaustion and grief, John tried not to picture his beloved Hetch Hetchy meadows and stands of oak and pine trees under water. He coughed constantly and battled a lung infection. He told his worried daughters that he was tired, but would continue his "pen work" and finish *Travels in Alaska*.

The following year at the age of 76, John set about restoring his home. After clearing out the old furnishings, he bought new furniture and, to everyone's amazement, installed electricity. He hired a secretary and worked 12-hour days. At the end of each day, he stored his Alaskan manuscript in an orange crate. Then he walked down the road to eat at the adobe house with Wanda, Tom, and their now four lively sons.

In midsummer, World War I broke out in Europe. John was so upset that he could not talk or write about it, except to Wanda. He worried about the European friends he had met over the years. He sent a generous check to the Red Cross to aid the people of Belgium.

On December 3, he wrote to Helen that "everything [in the house] has been put in comparative order." His chronic cough grew worse. A few days later, he took the train south to Daggett, arriving in the early dawn as a bitterly cold wind swept across the Mojave Desert. Although he caught a cold, he was excited to see Helen, Buel, and the children, including his seventh grandson, Richard, born that summer.

Before long, John's cold turned into pneumonia and he had to be hospitalized 80 miles (130 km) away in Los Angeles. He died in the early hours of December 24, 1914. His Alaskan manuscript lay on his hospital bed waiting to be revised.

"The Mountains are calling me and I must go."

*John pauses beside the Merced River in his beloved Yosemite.
Beyond him are the royal arches of North Dome.*

John in Muir Woods

Epilogue

I only went out for a walk and finally concluded to
stay out till sundown, for going out, I found, was really
going in.

Honoring their father's wishes, Wanda and Helen buried
John in the family plot in Martinez, beside their mother, Louie.

After learning of John Muir's death, John Burroughs
wrote in his journal that it is "an event that I have been ex-
pecting and dreading....A unique character—greater as a
talker than a writer...I shall greatly miss him."

Travels in Alaska, one of John's 10 major books, was
published in 1915. His books, essays, letters, and journals
continue to be published around the world in new editions
and collections.

On August 25, 1916, the National Park Service was established, immediately taking charge of Yosemite and 34
other national parks in the West. Rangers wearing the familiar
gray and green uniform, gold badge, and distinctive hat now
preside over 350 parks, monuments, seashores, rivers, and
preserves covering 80 million acres (32 million hectares).
More than 250 million people from around the world visit one
or more national parks each year. Besides Yosemite, these
include such places as the White House, Civil War battlefields,
the Grand Canyon, and spots along both coasts.

Hundreds of geographical features from Alaska to
Dunbar, Scotland, in addition to streets and buildings, bear
the name of John Muir. Part of the Wisconsin farmland that
the famous naturalist tramped through as a boy is now a historical site. The Muir Woods National Monument, established
in 1908, lies north of San Francisco. A trail loops through

several hundred acres of coastal redwoods—land that John often explored as a young man when he needed to escape San Francisco for a few hours.

The John Muir National Historic Site is east of San Francisco in Martinez, California. This park includes part of the Strentzels' fruit ranch and surrounds the Victorian house of John and Louie Muir and some of the other original buildings. Visitors can see John Muir's "scribble den" on the second floor, climb to the tower above the third floor and ring the bell, or sample apples in the orchard.

California's governor proclaims each April 21 "John Muir Day," in honor of John Muir's birthday. Each year, hundreds of people picnic on the grounds of the John Muir National Historical Site and enjoy marching bagpipers and Scottish highland dancers. Some, including John's ten grandchildren, are direct descendants of the Muir family. Many wear Scottish tartan kilts. It's not hard to imagine John Muir on the lawn, tapping and twirling to the familiar cadence of drum and pipe, dressed in a kilt of his family's green and black Gordon tartan.

One hundred years after its creation, the Sierra Club remains at the forefront of environmental action by helping to preserve additional wilderness areas. From its headquarters in San Francisco, the club sponsors outdoor adventures around the world, and programs about natural history. The Sierra Club also works actively to influence policies and decisions affecting the environment. Four hundred chapters or groups exist today in the United States and Canada, with more than 650,000 members.

Yosemite National Park covers approximately 1,200 square miles (3,100 square km) of meadows, mountains, cliffs, rivers, waterfalls, and glaciers. There are more than

700 miles (1,100 km) of trails and a variety of year-round activities, from rock climbing to bird watching. More than 3 million visitors travel to Yosemite National Park each year; 70 percent spend most of their time exploring the floor of the seven-mile (11 km)-long Yosemite Valley. There are several museums that display information about the Sierra Nevada, the early residents of the area, and John Muir.

Every year thousands of people hike and backpack throughout the mountains, enjoying the Sierra Nevada. Some walk along all or part of the John Muir Trail, which stretches 212 miles (341 km) along the crest of the high Sierra Nevada from Yosemite Valley to Mount Whitney. Completed in 1938, the popular trail is another memorial to John Muir.

Many historians consider John Muir the father of the national parks. Not only a scientist, writer, inventor, and mountaineer, he was also a visionary. In 1976 the California Historical Society voted John Muir the greatest Californian in the state's history.

His influence as a major figure in American history is not fading. If anything he is becoming more popular. His words are etched on walls and printed in books, but more importantly, John Muir's philosophy about wilderness and the earth's future lingers in the hearts and minds of us all.

> Climb the mountains and get their good tidings. Nature's peace will flow into you as sunshine flows into trees. The winds will blow their own freshness into you, and the storms their energy, while cares will drop off like autumn leaves.

Close-Up View of John Muir's Yosemite

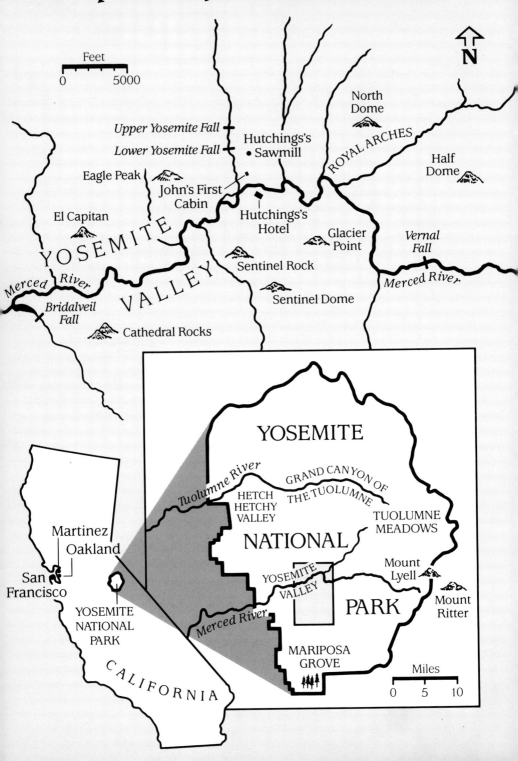

Feet

0   5000

N

Upper Yosemite Fall
Lower Yosemite Fall

Hutchings's
• Sawmill

North
Dome

ROYAL ARCHES

Half
Dome

Eagle Peak

John's First
Cabin

El Capitan

Hutchings's
Hotel

Glacier
Point

Vernal
Fall

Y O S E M I T E

Sentinel Rock

Merced River

V A L L E Y

Sentinel Dome

Merced River

Bridalveil
Fall

Cathedral Rocks

YOSEMITE

Tuolumne River

GRAND CANYON OF
THE TUOLUMNE

HETCH
HETCHY
VALLEY

TUOLUMNE
MEADOWS

Martinez
Oakland

NATIONAL

San
Francisco

YOSEMITE
VALLEY

Mount
Lyell

YOSEMITE
NATIONAL
PARK

Merced River

PARK

Mount
Ritter

C A L I F O R N I A

MARIPOSA
GROVE

Miles

0   5   10

Sources

p.9   John Muir, *The Story of My Boyhood and Youth* (Madison: University of Wisconsin Press, 1965), 11.

p.10   Linnie Marsh Wolfe, *Son of the Wilderness: The Life of John Muir* (Madison: University of Wisconsin Press, 1978), 14.

p.13   Muir, *Boyhood and Youth,* 42.

p.13   Ibid., 45.

p.15   Ibid., 47.

p.16   Ibid., 52-3.

p.18   Ibid., 177.

p.18   James Mitchell Clarke, *The Life and Adventures of John Muir* (San Francisco: Sierra Club Books, 1980), 18.

p.19   Wolfe, *Son of the Wilderness,* 34-5.

p.20   John Muir to James Whitehead, 1913, John Muir Papers, Holt-Atherton Center for Western Studies, University of the Pacific. Copyright © 1984 Muir-Hanna Trust. (Muir left many letters partly or wholly undated.)

p.20   Wolfe, *Son of the Wilderness,* 49.

p.23   Ibid., 45.

p.23   Ibid., 41.

p.25   Muir, *Boyhood and Youth,* 197.

p.26   John Muir to Mrs. Edward Pelton, 1861, Muir Papers.

p.26   Charles Reid to John Muir, 1860.

p.26   Wolfe, *Son of the Wilderness,* 48.

p.28   John Muir to Mary, Annie, and Joanna Muir, May 1861, Muir Papers.

p.32   James Whitehead to John Muir, 1913.

p.32   Anne Gilrye Muir to John Muir, 1862.

p.33   Muir journals, 1863.

p.33   John Muir to Emily Pelton, 1 March 1863.

p.35   John Muir to Jeanne Carr, 1866.

p.36   John Muir to Sarah Muir, May 1866.

p.37   Clarke, *John Muir,* 48.

p.37   John Muir, *A Thousand-Mile Walk to the Gulf* (Boston: Houghton Mifflin, 1981), xvi.

p.37   Muir journals, 1867, Muir Papers.

p.38   Clarke, *John Muir,* 50.

p.38   Wolfe, *Son of the Wilderness,* 107.

p.38   Clarke, *John Muir,* 51.

p.38   Muir, *Thousand-Mile Walk,* 2.

p.39   Ibid., ix.

p.40   Ibid., 14.

p.40   Ibid., 75-6.

p.40   Ibid., 70-1.

p.41   Ibid., 92.

p.43   Shirley Sargent, *John Muir in Yosemite* (Yosemite: Flying Spur Press, 1971), 9.

p.44   Muir, *Thousand-Mile Walk,* 191.

p.45   Sargent, *John Muir,* 10.

p.46   John Muir to Jeanne Carr, undated, Muir Papers.

p.46   Muir journals, 1868.

p.46   John Muir to David Muir, 1868.

p.46   Muir journals, 13 February 1869.

p.47   John Muir, *My First Summer in the Sierra* (San Francisco: Sierra Club Books, 1988), 10.
p.48   Ibid., 148.
p.51   John Muir to Sarah Muir, Summer 1869, Muir Papers.
p.51   Muir, *My First Summer,* 83.
p.53   Muir journals, undated, Muir Papers.
p.54   Muir, *My First Summer,* 110.
p.55   Therese Yelverton, *Zanita: A Tale of the Yosemite,* 29.
p.58   Clarke, *John Muir,* 96.
p.58   Joseph Le Conte, "Journal of Ramblings through the High Sierra of California," *Sierra Club Bulletin* III (January 1900).
p.58   John Muir to Jeanne Carr, 13 August 1871, Muir Papers.
p.61   Muir journals, undated fragment written after meeting Emerson.
p.61   S.S. Forbes to William Frederic Bade, 12 July 1915.
p.62   John Muir, "Living Glaciers of California," *Overland Monthly* IX (December 1872): 547-9.
p.62   John Muir, "Fountains and Streams of Yosemite National Park," *Atlantic Monthly* (April 1901).
p.63   Muir journals, undated, Muir Papers.
p.65   John Muir to Dan Beard, April 1907.
p.67   John Muir to Sarah Muir, 1873.
p.67   John Muir to Jeanne Carr, undated.
p.68   Muir journals, undated.
p.68   Muir journals, September 1875.
p.71   John Muir, *The Mountains of California* (New York: Penguin Books, 1985), 179.
p.73   John Muir, "The Hetch-Hetchy Valley," *Sierra Club Bulletin* (January 1908): 217.
p.76   Louisiana Strentzel diary, 17 June 1879, Muir Papers.
p.79   Frederick Turner, *Rediscovering America: John Muir in His Time and Ours* (San Francisco: Sierra Club Books, 1985), 259.
p.79   John Muir to General Bidwell, April 1880, Muir Papers.
p.81   Muir journals, undated.
p.83   John Muir to Mary Muir, October 1881.
p.88   Turner, *Rediscovering America,* 275.
p.89   John Muir to Louie Muir, 1888, Muir Papers.
p.89   Louie Muir to John Muir, 9 August 1888.
p.90   Shirley Sargent, *Yosemite: The First 100 Years* (Santa Barbara: Sequoia Communications, 1988), 24.
p.91   *Oakland Tribune,* 16 September 1890.
p.93   Samuel Merrill, "Personal Recollections of John Muir," *Sierra Club Bulletin* XIII (17 July 1927): 24-30.
p.97   Jean Hanna Muir and Shirley Sargent, eds., *Dear Papa: Letters Between John Muir and His Daughter Wanda* (Fresno: Panorama West Books, 1985), 8.
p.97   Ibid., 28.
p.98   John Muir to Louie Muir, Spring 1893, Muir Papers.
p.100   John Muir to Robert Underwood Johnson, undated.
p.100   Jean Hanna Muir and Shirley Sargent, *Dear Papa,* 47.
p.101   Wolfe, *Son of the Wilderness,* 269.
p.101   Michael P. Cohen, *The Pathless Way: John Muir and American Wilderness* (Madison: University of Wisconsin Press, 1984), 193.
p.101   John Muir to Louie Muir, undated, Muir Papers.

p.103 John Muir, "The American Forests," *Atlantic Monthly* (August 1897).

p.104 Ibid.

p.104 John Muir, "The Wild Parks and Forest Reservations of the West," *Atlantic Monthly* (January 1898).

p.107 John Muir to Louie Muir, Autumn 1898, Muir Papers.

p.107 John Muir to Charles Sargent, 1898.

p.108 John Muir to Katherine Graydon, October 1901.

p.109 John Muir to Louie Muir, 20 July 1901.

p.110 Theodore Roosevelt's first address to Congress, December 1901.

p.110 Theodore Roosevelt to John Muir, 14 March 1903.

p.112 John Muir to William Trout, undated.

p.112 Theodore Roosevelt to John Muir, 19 May 1903.

p.112 Theodore Roosevelt's California addresses, 1903.

p.113 John Muir to Louie Muir, undated.

p.115 Muir journals, 1905.

p.115 C. Hart Merriam, "To the Memory of John Muir," *Sierra Club Bulletin* X (January 1917): 146-51.

p.124 John Muir to Robert Underwood Johnson, September 1907, Muir Papers.

p.124 John Muir to William Colby, 1908.

p.126 Joanna Muir to John Muir, undated.

p.127 Muir journals, August 1912.

p.127 Ibid., January 1912.

p.128 Ibid., December 1912.

p.129 Wolfe, *Son of the Wilderness,* 337.

p.129 John Muir, *The Yosemite* (San Francisco: Sierra Club Books, 1988), 261-2.

p.129 John Muir to Henry Osborn, July 1913, Muir Papers.

p.129 John Muir to Helen Muir, 15 November 1913.

p.130 John Muir to Helen Muir, 3 December 1913.

p.130 Muir journals, September 1873.

p.133 John Muir, *John of the Mountains: The Unpublished Journals of John Muir,* ed. Linnie Marsh Wolfe (Boston: Houghton Mifflin, 1938).

p.133 Paul Brooks, *Speaking for Nature* (San Francisco: Sierra Club Books, 1983), 30.

p.135 John Muir, "Yellowstone National Park," *Atlantic Monthly* (April 1898).

Bibliography

Writings by John Muir

John of the Mountains: The Unpublished Journals of John Muir. Edited by Linnie Marsh Wolfe. Boston: Houghton Mifflin, 1938.

The Mountains of California. New York: Penguin Books, 1985.

My First Summer in the Sierra. San Francisco: Sierra Club Books, 1988.

Our National Parks. Madison: University of Wisconsin Press, 1981.

Stickeen. Berkeley: Heyday Books, 1990.

The Story of My Boyhood and Youth. Madison: University of Wisconsin Press, 1965.

A Thousand-Mile Walk to the Gulf. Boston: Houghton Mifflin, 1981.

Travels in Alaska. San Francisco: Sierra Club Books, 1988.

The Yosemite. San Francisco: Sierra Club Books, 1988.

Papers. Holt-Atherton Center for Western Studies, University of the Pacific, Stockton, California. Copyright © 1984 Muir-Hanna Trust.

Other Sources

Badé, Frederick. *The Life and Letters of John Muir.* 2 vols. Boston: Houghton Mifflin, 1924.

Brooks, Paul. *Speaking for Nature.* San Francisco: Sierra Club Books, 1983.

Browning, Peter, ed. *John Muir in His Own Words.* Walnut Creek, California: Great West Books, 1988.

Clarke, James Mitchell. *The Life and Adventures of John Muir.* San Francisco: Sierra Club Books, 1980.

Cohen, Michael. *The Pathless Way: John Muir and the American Wilderness.* Madison: University of Wisconsin Press, 1984.

Emanuels, George. *John Muir Inventor.* Fresno: Panorama West Books, 1985.

Engberg, Robert, ed. *John Muir: Summering in the Sierra.* Madison: University of Wisconsin Press, 1984.

Farquhar, Francis. *History of the Sierra Nevada.* Berkeley: University of California Press, 1966.

Fox, Stephen. *John Muir and His Legacy: The American Conservation Movement.* Boston: Little, Brown, 1981.

Kimes, William and Maymie. *John Muir: A Reading Bibliography.* Fresno: Panorama West Books, 1986.

Limbaugh, Ronald H., and Kirsten E. Lewis, eds. *The Guide and Index to the Microform Edition of the John Muir Papers, 1858-1957.* Alexandria, Virginia: Chadwyck-Healey, 1986.

Mighetto, Lisa, ed. *Muir Among the Animals: The Wildlife Writings of John Muir.* San Francisco: Sierra Club Books, 1986.

Muir, Jean Hanna, and Shirley Sargent, eds. *Dear Papa: Letters Between John Muir and His Daughter Wanda.* Fresno: Panorama West Books, 1985.

Muir, John. National Historic Site, Martinez, California.

Nash, Roderick. *Wilderness and the American Mind.* New Haven: Yale University Press, 1967.

Sanborn, Margaret. *Yosemite: Its Discovery, Its Wonders, and Its People.* Yosemite: Yosemite Association, 1989.

Sargent, Shirley. *John Muir In Yosemite.* Yosemite: Flying Spur Press, 1971.

————. *Yosemite: The First 100 Years.* Santa Barbara: Sequoia Communications, 1988.

Strong, Douglas. *Dreamers and Defenders: American Conservationists.* Lincoln: University of Nebraska Press, 1971.

Turner, Frederick. *Rediscovering America, John Muir in His Times and Ours.* San Francisco: Sierra Club Books, 1985.

Wolfe, Linnie Marsh. *Son of the Wilderness, The Life of John Muir.* Madison: University of Wisconsin Press, 1978.

Yosemite National Park Research Library, Yosemite, California. Assorted papers.

Index

(Numbers in **bold face** refer to illustrations)

143

Photo Acknowledgments

The illustrations have been reproduced through the courtesy of: pp. 1, 6, 11, 14 (top), 19, 21, 31, 33, 34, 36, 42, 44, 48, 51, 52, 54, 56, 63, 64, 66, 69, 71, 77, 78, 79, 80, 83, 84, 85, 86, 87, 88, 92, 93, 94, 96, 98, 99, 103, 105, 108, 109, 114, 116, 117, 118, 120, 122, 125, 128, 132, John Muir Papers, Holt-Atherton Special Collections, University of the Pacific Libraries, © 1984 Muir-Hanna Trust; pp. 2, 45, 47, 49, 50, 59, 60, 111, 131, Yosemite National Park Research Library; pp. 14 (bottom), 24, 29, 75, State Historical Society of Wisconsin; pp. 30, 39, 123, Library of Congress; pp. 70, 106, Bancroft Library; pp. 74, 119, John Muir National Historic Site; p. 102, California Section, California State Library; p. 136, Laura Westlund.
Front cover photo courtesy of John Muir Papers, Holt-Atherton Special Collections, University of the Pacific Libraries, © 1984 Muir-Hanna Trust.
Back cover photo courtesy of Yosemite collections, National Park Service.

Page 1: This photo of John Muir at Bullfrog Lake was taken on a Sierra Club outing in 1908.

Page 2: John stands with Helen's dog Stickeen at the Martinez ranch.